C000104081

RUGBY LEAGUE
Where Are They Now?

Autumn 2007

Published by
yfppublishing.com

**Written &
Researched
by**
John Huxley

High tackles inserted by
Les Rowley

Cover designed by
Chris Womersley

All photographs by
Andrew Varley

Printed by
Duffields Printers, Leeds

Copyright © 2007 YFP Publishing
ISBN
978-0-9545333-6-6

Former Players

Mick Adams
Kevin Ashcroft
Willie Aspinall
Paul Atcheson
John Atkinson
Bob Beardmore
Kevin Beardmore
Keith Bell
John Bentley
Billy Benyon
Denis Betts
John Bevan
Paul Bishop
Tommy Bishop
Reg Bowden
Eddie Bowman
Keith Bridges
Ian Brooke
Chris Burton
Len Casey
Dave Chisnall
Colin Clarke
Phil Clarke
Terry Clawson

Gary Connolly
Gerald Cordle
Kel Coslett
Andy Currier
John Dalgreen
Jonathan Davies
John Devereux
Kevin Dick
Roy Dickinson
Gary Divorty
Paul Dixon
Steve Donlan
Des Drummond
Ray Dutton
Les Dyl
Paul Eastwood
Shaun Edwards
Keith Elwell
Steve Evans
Richie Eyres
George Fairbairn
Karl Fairbank
Vince Farrar

Keith Fielding
Tony Fisher
Terry Flanaghan
Adam Fogerty
Mike Ford
Colin Forsyth
Deryck Fox
Neil Fox
Mick George
Scott Gibbs
Henderson Gill
Parry Gordon
Andy Goodway
Peter Gorley
Bobbie Goulding
Ken Gowers
Jeff Grayshon
Clive Griffiths
Jonathan Griffiths
Adrian Hadley
Steve Hampson
Ellery Hanley
Alan Hardisty
Paul Harkin

Neil Harmon
Brendan Hill
Phil Hogan
Neil Holding
Les Holliday
John Holmes
Terry Holmes
Eric Hughes
David Hulme
Paul Hulme
Lee Jackson
John Joyner
Chris Joynt
Tony Karalius
Ken Kelly
Paddy Kirwan
Phil Larder
Brian Lockwood
Paul Loughlin
Phil Lowe
Ian Lucas
Joe Lydon
Barrie McDermott
John Mantle
Jim Mills
Roger Millward
Mick Morgan
Keith Mumby
Craig Murdock
Alex Murphy
Martin Murphy

Tony Myler
Steve Nash
Paul Newlove
Mike Nicholas
George Nicholls
Martin Offiah
Steve O'Neill
Geoff Pimblett
Harry Pinner
Steve Pitchford
Andy Platt
Scott Quinnell
Dave Redfearn
Malcolm Reilly
Dean Sampson
Garry Schofield
Glyn Shaw
Kelvin Skerrett
Trevor Skerrett
Alan Smith
Kurt Sorensen
Gary Stephens
Nigel Stephenson
Mike Stephenson

Anthony Sullivan
Clive Sullivan
Mick Sullivan
Eddie Syzmah
Ray Tabern
Jimmy Thompson
David Topliss
Ian Van Bellen
Kevin Ward
Edward Marsden
Waring
David Watkins
Dave Watkinson
Derek Whitehead
John Woods

We wish to acknowledge the following people without whom the production of this book would have been almost impossible:

Neil Atkinson (Huddersfield Examiner),
David Burke (Daily Telegraph)
Frank Cassidy (North West Evening Mail),
Phil Clarke (SkySports),
Pat Cluskey (Widnes Vikings RLFC),
Rob Cole(Westgate Sports, Cardiff),
Mrs Carolyn Evans of Chorley
Raymond Fletcher (RFL Statistician),
Derek Hallas (Leeds Ex-Players),
Roger Halstead (Oldham Ex-Players),
John Kendrew (Castleford Ex-Players),
John Kidd (Swinton Lions),
Keith Mills (Wigan Warriors RLFC),
Martin Morgan (Whitehaven News),
George Nicholls (Widnes Ex-Players),
David Parker (League Weekly),
Geoff Pimblett (St Helens Ex-Players),
Mike Stephenson (SkySports),
George Thornton (Warrington Wolves Ex-Players),
Richard Tingle (Hull FC),
David Howes
Mr Google
Christopher Irvine
Harry Edgar

All stand for
the
Author's foreword

During what amounts to a working lifetime in and around Rugby League, one thing has remained constant, my admiration for the men who played in the professional game. Their athletic prowess; their courage and, in most cases, their modesty is amazing and, without question, they are to a man remarkable people.

With each succeeding generation new men step up to play their part to not only entertain the sport many, and fortunately growing legion of fans, but also to prove their worth as both competitors and athletes of real quality in one of the most demanding team games yet devised by men.

It is now more than 40 years since I first entered The Willows to watch my first live game of Rugby League, Salford v Swinton, and, during that time, I have been fortunate to meet many of this special breed of men while working as a Rugby League journalist and later as an administrator.

As the years rolled by I started to wonder what had happened to many of those heroes, villains and stars that had emerged during my lifetime within the sport.

That curiosity was provided with an outlet thanks to the decision of Andrew Varley and Les Rowley of **yfppublishing.com** to publish this volume.

To them I would like to extend thanks for the opportunity to write about these players again and to re-awaken many valuable friendships. It has been a very rewarding experience and I hope that the readers will enjoy reading about what happened to their former heroes as much as I did researching their lives.

The list of players we chose to research was totally arbitrary: it comprised, in general, of players we knew and admired. We make no apologies for that method of selection.

So, dear reader, we hope that you enjoy the journey of re-discovery as much as we did. Every effort has been made to ensure the facts we have mentioned within the book are accurate, but if any errors have slipped through the net, I take full responsibility for them.

John Huxley
Autumn 2007

A few words from Garry Schofield OBE...

Rugby League prides itself on being a family game and those of us who have been fortunate enough to have played the sport as professionals belong to a family within a family.

The sharing of triumph and disaster, pain and joy as well as all the sheer hard work, ensures that, with few exceptions, you establish a special bond with the other players.

For most of us that bond will be life-long and, even though we may no longer see each other either as team mates or as opposing players, that fellowship link remains in place.

Of course you simply can't keep tabs on everybody, there are just too many players in Rugby League at any one time for that, and that's why 'Where Are They Now – Rugby League' is going to be so valuable to both fans and former players alike.

Once you finish your playing career, life beckons. Some players opt to stay close to Rugby League, while others select careers and lifestyles very different from the days when they featured in the sporting headlines.

For some there has been success; for others the injuries sustained during their playing careers have subsequently seriously impacted in their lives while others have left Britain behind.

It has been fascinating to read what players from so many different generations did once they put their boots away for the last time and I am sure that this book will provide us all with not only hours of entertainment but also give sports quiz question writers a whole load of new material with which to tease us for years to come.

Happy reading

Garry Schofield OBE

Mick Adams

Age: 56.
Born: Widnes.
Clubs: Widnes, Canterbury-Bankstown (Australia).
Playing Era: 1969 – 1984.
Position: Loose forward.
Style: Clever footballer with pace. Not the biggest forward in the game but intelligent with it.
Star turn: One of the great influences on the Widnes team that dominated the Challenge Cup competition throughout the 1970s and early 1980s.
Retirement: His great mate was former Chemics forward Dave Macko who died prematurely of a brain haemorrhage. They buried Dave the day before Widnes played in the 1984 Challenge Cup Final and the effect was that Mick decided to finish as a player after that Wembley appearance.

What happened then? He packed up everything and emigrated to Australia.
Why Australia? When he was on tour with Great Britain in 1979 Mick took some time out to get married. His bride, Chris, was a *sheila* he had met earlier and for the wedding Eric Hughes was best man whilst some of his other team mates were the groomsmen.
I'll bet that was some stag do: A bricklayer by trade, when Mick played at Widnes he worked for Halton Borough Council as a labourer then went in to a supervisory role.
Australian working life: When he landed in Tamworth (Tammi), New South Wales – that's his wife's hometown – he started where he left off in England by becoming a brickie's mate. But after he became established he went to work for the Australian distribution company TNT and ended up buying a truck to deliver parcels around the region.
Switched industries: Then, 13 years ago, he moved into the transport industry working for a company that sourced spare parts for trucks and trailers. And that's what he's doing today.
Pommie bashing: He's known as a Parts Interpreter but his customers still call him a 'Pom'.

Kevin Ashcroft

Age: 63. Born on D-Day in 1944.
Born: Newton-le-Willows.
Sounds fancy: It's between Leigh and St. Helens.
Clubs: Dewsbury, Rochdale Hornets, Leigh, Warrington, Salford.
Playing era: 1963 – 1985.
Retirement due to: Injury. In those days he had his poll tax demand sent straight to Leigh Infirmary. Today it's his council tax with both knees replaced; an elbow joint replaced as well as operations on his ankle, Achilles tendon and his thumb...and all because he played rugby league.

Does he still work? Hardly.
So no rugby league pounds swelling the coffers? A couple of years ago he went as an advisor to Blackpool Panthers but now he's just an interested fan.
What did he do for a living before he retired? Kev spent most of his working life in engineering and spent many years working for the late Warrington chairman Brian Pitchford at Locker Industries in Warrington.
What else did he do? Well like many other ex-players he had a pub for a while, the Albion in Atherton near Leigh. Then he worked on and off for Leigh Rugby League Club until his health forced him to take a back seat.
Voice: Mind you Kev might have been out of the game for some time but you can still hear him. His outspoken views on Rugby League mean that Manchester Evening News and BBC Radio Manchester have sought him out to be a pundit on many occasions. And Kev isn't afraid of saying what he feels about the game and has the nickname 'Controversial Kev'.
Is he controversial? He told the entire Salford team as recently as August 2007 to 'buck their ideas up'. That's great coming from an ex-coach.
Does he have a media catch phrase yet? Oh yes. It's *"Couldn't agree with you more"*.
Would I recognise him today? He wears large 70s style glasses that weigh more than his head and likes the big coats.

Willie Aspinall

Age: The Beatles sang about it and we will still love you.
Born: St Helens.
Clubs: Warrington, Rochdale Hornets.
Era: 1962 – 1976.
Position: Scrum half

How come he ended up with Warrington and not Saints? Willie was a very laid back individual – and still is! But when it came to joining his home-town club it didn't appeal to him because he knew too many people at Knowsley Road.
Working life: Willie was a fitter by trade but after a chance meeting in 1979 with former internationals Jack Wilkinson and Brian Briggs, both of whom had pubs in Wakefield, decided to go into the licensed trade.
Oh, how interesting: He had three pubs in and around St Helens. The Unicorn in Billinge, the Rams Head in Haydock and, finally, The Eagle and Child in Rainford.
Today: Willie is semi-retired and has found himself a tidy little number working on the ground staff at Grange Park Golf Club.
A divot replacement officer? *"I love the job, but there's just one draw back – getting up at 5.30am to start work!"*
Not on his Christmas Card list: Alex Murphy. After nine and half years at Warrington, he found himself surplus to requirements following Alex's arrival from Leigh so he signed for Rochdale Hornets.
Did he stay there for long? Until 1976 when he found first team places hard to come by and then he retired.
Action! During his playing career Willie was a keen cine cameraman and he has a collection of films taken in Australia and New Zealand when he was a member of the 1966 Great Britain tour party as well as when he was playing with both his professional clubs.
Wow: He's joined them altogether and is intending to transfer them to video or DVD.
What a great Christmas present for my old Uncle Cedric.
When is it out? Not this year.

Paul Atcheson

Age: 34.

A mere whippersnapper: Shame really but Paul became disillusioned with the game.

Born: Ormskirk, Lancashire

Clubs: Widnes (twice), Wigan, Oldham, St Helens.

Look-alike: Bobby Davro.

Position: Full back.

Nickname: Patch.

Quit: He made the decision to call it a day a week before he got married and while on the way back from a heavy defeat at Castleford and decided his heart wasn't in it.

Working life: Up until he became a full-time player with Wigan he had been training to work in electronics with a company that dealt with TV, radio and audio repairs. But they wanted him to study at night school for the qualifications he needed and that didn't go along with being a semi-professional rugby league player.

Now what does he do? He's a drayman with Carlsberg UK and works alongside his former St Helens team-mate Tommy Martyn.

Plenty of perks? *"It's a great job and the trade has changed even during the two years I've been working in it."*

You mean he only gets to drink two pints at each pub he delivers to? The job is about workload and delivery of service these days. He gets an allowance but he takes it home to the missus.

The Welsh wizard: It was emotional putting the Welsh international jersey on for the first time. His mum is Welsh, which is how he qualified for the Dragons and he was part of a Welsh team that beat England at Ninian Park, Cardiff in 1995.

Mates: Paul stays in touch with his pal Dion Bird, the former Paris St Germain, Hull and Widnes back as well as New Zealand prop Julian O'Neill who played for St Helens and Widnes.

New technology: *"E-mail's a wonderful aid to keeping friendships alive".*

Is he on Facebook? He's more a YouTube man.

John Atkinson

Age: 60
Born: Leeds
Clubs: Leeds, Carlisle
Era: 1965 – 1982
Position: Winger
Game style: Aggressive and speedy. He knew where the try line was and there was no messing with John. A tough cookie.
Union dues: Although John came from a family with a great League background, he joined Leeds from the former Roundhay Rugby Union Club. He'd gone to a union playing school and his Dad wasn't too keen on him playing amateur league in those days.

Work: John served an apprenticeship as a joiner and used to work for the GPO – the Post Office.
Did he build beds for people to sleep in when they were queueing for their dole money? Now, now, it never got that bad. Then he joined the police force and still is a serving officer.
At 60? Yes, but he doesn't run after crimbos like he did in his younger days. He's mainly doing desk duties.
The pen is the new baton: Exactly.
Have you mentioned 1970 yet? At Leeds he played on the opposite wing to Alan Smith. Together they formed a lethal strike force for Great Britain and were members of the last Lions team to beat Australia both, Down Under, and in any Test series since 1970.
Caps: 26.
Connections: For the last six years John has been a serving member on the RFL's Disciplinary Advisory Panel. You get sin-binned for a punch on the field and six months suspended off it. Best leave the fisticuffs for during matches, eh?
Shirt number: 5.
Criminals nicked: 100s.
Mates: John and Alan Smith have stuck together and they see each other and their families on a regular basis.
Now lives: North Yorkshire.

Bob Beardmore

Okay, which one is he? He's the one with the bushy hair and a light tanned moustache.

As opposed to...? the one with the bushy hair and a light tanned moustache.

Age: 47

Clubs: Castleford, Leigh Scarborough Pirates.

Era: 1978 – 1992

Style: Busy as a bee behind the scrum. He combined pace with craft.

Can I tell them apart today? Well, let's put it this way: Bob stayed in sport after his Rugby League days were over and kept himself fit, while Kevin, who was born ten minutes before Bob, went into pub life: likes a pint and a smoke.

Say no more: Bob went back to his first love, soccer.

Which club did he play for? He played for the New Airedale Hotel team and if that sounds familiar it's because his brother Kevin is the landlord.

How did he do? Beers on the house on more than one occasion.

Work: Bob served an apprenticeship as a maintenance fitter but today he's a Technical Manager with a crane manufacturing company.

So he's going up in the world? He doesn't go up in them much these days.

Highlights: For Bob it never got much better than playing for Castleford in the 1986 Challenge Cup Final at Wembley when they beat Hull KR 15-14 and he won the Lance Todd Trophy as Man of the Match.

Did you know? He once scored 38 points in one game.

Kevin Beardmore

Funny name. Did he have more beard than anyone else? No.
Age: 47
Born: Cas.
Clubs: Cas. A one man club.
Playing era: 1977 – 1999
Game style: In your face hooker wearing a headband. Aggressive, fast and assertive. Also confusing, his identical twin Bob was also the side's scrum half.
Retirement: End of the 1999 season.
On the coal face of sport: While Kevin was playing for

Castleford he was a miner and worked at Fryston Colliery. That was until the end of the national miners' strike in 1984 and then, like many a rugby player before him, Kevin took a pub.
And today? 19 years on and he's still the landlord at the New Airedale Hotel in Castleford.
Does he regale stories of the old days to rugby mad Cas fans? His sporting passion is football these days. Liverpool Football Club to be precise.
How keen is he? Very. Kevin's a season ticket holder at Anfield and he follows the Liverpool team both home and away. He doesn't miss a game.
Blimey, that is serious: Besides being a fan, he sells Liverpool lottery tickets in his boozer which entitles him to two extra tickets a week.
So when Liverpool play Pontefract Working Mens I know where to go for tickets. Do many of the players go to his pub? Former defender Alan Kennedy has nipped in and he's been in the company of Danish midfielder Jan Molby when they were both at the National Sports Centre at Lilleshall.
Rugby highlights: Playing in the Challenge Cup Final in 1986 when Cas started as underdogs and beat Hull KR. That was the game when Australian Aboriginal winger Jamie Sandy captured all the headlines as Malcolm Reilly's Cas triumphed.

Keith Bell

DOB: 15 September 1953
Born: Featherstone
Clubs: Featherstone Rovers, Hunslet.
The glamour clubs? You take what you can get.
Retirement: 1993
Position: Loose forward
The Rovers return: Keith was the fifth member of his family to sign for the Rovers.
Working life: He was an apprentice at the glassworks in neighbouring Knottingley and later became a contractor on the near by power stations.
**It was a funny ol' game back

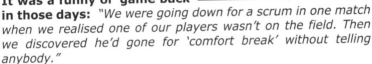

in those days:** *"We were going down for a scrum in one match when we realised one of our players wasn't on the field. Then we discovered he'd gone for 'comfort break' without telling anybody."*
Who was it? Keith's not naming him.
In the end: Keith finished his career with a two and half year spell with Hunslet but he had to finish playing because of the deteriorating state of his hip.
I guess golfers get the yips and players get the hips: Such was the pain he was in, he had to give up his fitting contract on the power stations and he worked for a little time in some warehouses in Featherstone. Subsequently he had his hip replaced in 1998.
Coaching: He was in charge at Featherstone Lions for quite some time but now spends his time assisting with the club's administration and management.
Bad luck: Keith was granted a testimonial by the Rugby Football League but there were so many players at Featherstone who also qualified for a benefit that by the time Keith's turn came around it was 1983-84 season. And what did that coincide with? The national miners' strike.
Doh! *"Featherstone was a coal mining village, nobody had any money so my testimonial wasn't very successful."*
Today: Retired and living in Featherstone.

John Bentley

DOB: 1967.
Born: Dewsbury.
Clubs: Leeds, Halifax, Balmain (Australia), Huddersfield
Position: Wing.
Playing era: 1988 – 1999
Nickname: Bentos.
Code switch: Although John was born in West Yorkshire he made a name for himself in union playing for Sale and England.
Take no prisoners: John had a very aggressive style of playing. He used to scare his own shadow.
Flying squad: John came into

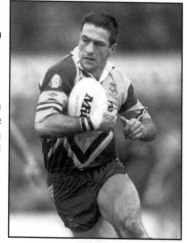

the game via the police. *"That caused problems both on and off the pitch. In matches it was seen as the only legal way to plant one on a police officer and off the pitch I got plenty of verbal abuse."*

Career break: John took a sabbatical from the Police to pursue his full-time playing career. When it was time to go back on the beat he chose rugby.

Back to union: When union went professional in 1995, John was tempted from league and signed a two-year contract with Newcastle Falcons. His impact on union was instant and he was included on the 1997 British Lions tour of South Africa where he ended up on the winning side but was accused by a disappointed South African of gouging.

The dark side couldn't keep him: After playing for England rugby union twice more, John joined Halifax but guess what...? He went back to union again.

What was he doing! Such a good job at the Galpharm Stadium that Leeds Tykes rugby union club offered him a job in development and he took it. And he's still working for the Headingley Carnegie union outfit.

What does he develop? His actual title is Community Marketing Manager and he has two people working under him who help put on camps and facilities for youngsters to get involved. Bentos takes charge of the kids and they love him.

Billy Benyon

Age: 62.
Born: St Helens.
Clubs: St Helens, Warrington, Cronulla (Australia).
Era: 1961 – 1982.
Position: Centre three quarter/ stand off half.
Reputation: You didn't mess about with Billy and he certainly left his mark when tackling.
Pact: Billy and his mate Parry Gordon had a pact. They promised each other that they would say something if they ever thought the other wasn't pulling his weight in the team and that it was time to quit.

Never came to it: In the end Parry didn't have to tell Billy who had suffered an ankle injury in a Premiership semi-final against Hull KR. It took that long to heal that Billy retired as a player to concentrate on his coaching career.

Part-time coach. In spite of the fact that Billy coached Warrington, his home town club St Helens, Leigh and Swinton he never went into the profession full-time and kept his job all the way through his time in league.

It must have been a cracking job! Billy had an apprenticeship as a joiner and then became a general foreman in the building trade. So that's where he got his man management skills and there's definitely no place for softies on a building site.

And today: Now Billy works for St Helens Council where he is an Assistant Surveyor.

Today's game: Billy's not a regular visitor to modern Rugby League games. He's like so many other former players who haven't really taken to the modern style of playing the game.

Why not? *"It seems to me that there's just one way of playing the game and players are not allowed to express themselves."*

Sport: During the summer Billy brings out his golf clubs and enjoys a round or two.

Denis Betts

DOB: 14 July 1969.
That's Bastille Day: Not in Leigh it isn't.
Clubs: Wigan (twice), Auckland Warriors
Playing era: 1986 – 2001
Position: Second row forward
Soccer mad: He was a central defender with the Manchester United under-15 team before deciding to concentrate on his rugby. He could have been the next Steve Bruce.

Kiwi experience: When former Wigan coach John Monie left Central Park to take up a position as head coach with the new franchise in the Australian League, Auckland Warriors in New Zealand, he took both Great Britain internationals Denis and Andy Platt with him from Wigan. But both players subsequently returned to the UK and Denis went back to pick up the threads of his career at Wigan.

Cabinet room: Six championships, seven Challenge Cups, three Premierships, four John Player/Regal Trophies and two Lancashire Cups as well as the Lance Todd Trophy (1991) and the Man of Steel (1995).

These newer guys never have proper jobs like asphalt contractors anymore do they? No, he joined Wigan's coaching staff and was eventually appointed assistant coach to Mike Gregory in July 2003.

I remember that: He took temporary charge of the side when Mike Gregory was taken ill and held the position for a year before being moved sideways to make room for new head coach Australian Ian Millward. That did not sit comfortably with Denis who resigned in 2005.

Union bound: In January 2006 Denis moved out of Rugby League and into rugby union when he was appointed as skills and development coach with English Premiership club Gloucester.

Trivia reminder: Denis Betts scored the first try when rugby league made its debut at the JJB Stadium after their move across from Central Park.

John Bevan

Age: 56
Born: The Rhondda, Wales.
Club: Warrington
Era: 1973 – 1985
Position: Wing and centre.
Now lives: Monmouth.

How come he ended up in Rugby League? As a union man he couldn't find work easy to come by. When a number of League clubs came in for him, he jumped at the chance.

Why Warrington? Their scout was Welsh too.

Was he a success? The strong running Bevan took to rugby league like the proverbial duck

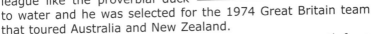

to water and he was selected for the 1974 Great Britain team that toured Australia and New Zealand.

Working life in League: The big incentive to come north from Wales was Warrington's offer to broker a teaching job and he went to work at Culcheth High School and then English Martyrs in Warrington where he was Head of PE and also a religious education teacher.

Independence: Two years before the end of his league playing career he was appointed to Arnold Public School in Blackpool as a PE teacher. He went back to union too, unfortunately.

Re-joining the Welsh union: John left teaching to join the Welsh union as Coaching Director. He also held other posts including assistant coach of the national side and coach of the under-19 team as well as their elite squad.

Back to teaching: Finally in 2000 he was appointed as a House Master at Monmouth School where he is a religious education teacher and works with their rugby players.

Embarrassment: Being breathalysed on the way home from his own testimonial bash in Warrington. The crystals went green but he'd been drinking brown ale - he couldn't understand it.

I'm a Magners man myself. Do you like it on ice? No, I always spill it when I get my skates on.

Paul Bishop

DOB: 5 July 1967, Warrington.
Clubs: Warrington, St Helens, Halifax, Cronulla, St George
Playing era: 1984 – 1994
Position: Scrum half.
Size: 5ft 6-ish.

Chip off the old block: Paul was destined to be a Rugby League star as he is the son of Tommy Bishop, the former Great Britain scrum half.

Working life: When Paul was starting his working life he lived in Keswick in Cumbria because his dad was coaching Workington Town and managed a pub in the town. He trained as a chef but left that behind when he became a full-time player with Warrington.

What does he think of Gordon Ramsay? He's got good ball handling skills but wouldn't pull his weight in the scrum.

Great moments: Paul still believes his two trips to play in Challenge Cup finals at Wembley were the greatest moments of his career even though he returned with losers' medals on each occasion.

What about all that hair? There was plenty of it and he didn't have that many trips to the hairdressers.

Why did he finish as a player? *"My knees and back were beginning to suffer so I decided that the time had come to call it a day."*

Lives: In the outback of Western Australia near Perth.

And earning a crust? Coaching Rugby League in the Western Australian town of Willagee.

Do they still play Rugby League in Western Australia? Yeah, they do now. At the start of the Super League era Western Reds were established in Perth but they didn't last for long, following Adelaide Rams into the history books.

New start: Willagee, the club that Paul is coaching, is one of eight clubs currently contesting a newly-established league competition.

Tommy Bishop

Age: 66
Born: St Helens
Clubs: Blackpool Borough, St Helens, Cronulla, Northern Suburbs (Brisbane).
Position: Scrum half
Era: 1959 – 1975.
Game style: Pint sized in stature but a giant sized footballer. Darting runs and great handling were his trademark.
Export: Tommy was selected for Great Britain's team that toured Australia and New Zealand in 1966 and he liked what he saw .
Beaches and sun? Something for the kids. After the 1968

World Cup Down Under, he told his club St Helens he was leaving.
New life: When he reached Australia he was appointed as captain-coach to Cronulla and one his first jobs was to lure St Helens' London-born Test prop Cliff Watson to join him. Together they helped inspire the Sharks to the 1973 Premiership Final where they were beaten 10-7 by Manly-Warringah. He followed that with a spell at Northern Suburbs in Brisbane, North Sydney and, finally, Cronulla again.
Retired: Aged 34.
Coaching: He coached Cronulla, Illawarra and North Sydney before returning to England to take over as coach at Workington Town. He later worked with both Leigh and Barrow before moving back to Australia in 1988.
Business: He ran a carpet cleaning enterprise and an orange juice business in Queensland. Today's he's retired and living in Robina on Queensland's Gold Coast.
They tell me it is wonderful out there: It is, but in the 80s the Japanese threw up too many high rises too close to the beaches and after 2pm they block out the sun on the sand. Not a bad thing if you're trying to get a bit of shade.
Face: Like leather.
Sons of rugby league: Paul played for Warrington and his Dad's club, St Helens.

Reg Bowden

Age: 57
Born: Widnes
Clubs: Widnes, Fulham and Warrington.
Playing era: 1972 – 1986
Nickname: The Clockwork Mouse.
Retired: What do you mean retired - He's still playing!
Get away: Reg has defied time by turning out for the Albert Park veterans in Widnes against a select side from younger players.
And he's still doing the business at scrum half? No, time has left its mark on Reg's body because he played in his last game as a prop.
Talent: Rated as one of the best English scrum halves never to be capped by Great Britain.
When did he finish as a professional? When he was 36 years old in 1986.
Why did he pack it in? *"When I could see what needed to be done and I just couldn't manage it myself. It was frustrating and spoiling it for me. That was when I decided to walk away."*
What was the best moment of his career? Reg's career at Widnes coincided with a golden era at Naughton Park so he found this question troublesome. In the end he plumped for his first Challenge Cup Final at Wembley in 1975. *"It was so new, so big and although I went back three more times, including as captain in 1979, it was so special that first time".*
What was it like playing with League legend Jim Mills? *"Jim was something special and I was playing alongside him in the games when he was sent off 21 times. I've often wondered whether it was something I said!"*
How has Reg earned his living since his playing days? For ten years he was in charge of Widnes's corporate entertaining packages and he also ran the club's lottery.
Licensed to thrill: Reg took possession of his own personal rugby league club. He bought the famous amateur club that had been formed by the late referee Mick Naughton, Widnes Tigers. Today it's called the Parklands Club.

Eddie Bowman

Age: 62.

Born: Whitehaven.

Position: Second row forward

Clubs: Whitehaven, Workington Town, Leigh, Wigan

Playing era: 1964 – 1979

Quit as a player: Eddie says he was like an old gunslinger who ran out of bullets.

The coaching manual: Eddie turned down Workington Town.

They're a bunch of amateurs: For a while after he finished playing Eddie coached a Whitehaven based amateur club. He spent seven years with them and stepped down gracefully after a job well done.

Working life: Originally Eddie was a fitter at Haig Colliery in Whitehaven. The pit's tunnels extended up to six miles out under the Irish Sea and Eddie worked there until it closed in 1964. Eddie then went to be an engineer at the atomic power station at Sellafield just down coast from Whitehaven. And he's still working there today.

Has he grown a spare head? Not yet.

Greatest memory: Being picked for the England team in the 1977 World Championship.

Survived: Eddie was one of the rare players who started his career with his home-town team Whitehaven but spent longer with their arch rivals just six miles up the West Cumbrian coast at Workington Town. Both towns call citizens from the other town 'jam-eaters' as a mark of disrespect.

Mate: If you see Eddie at a Rugby League game or function, it's odds on that not far away will be his pal Len Casey. The former Hull KR, Hull FC, Bradford and Wakefield forward has moved to take guest house in the Lake District and they both get together on a weekly basis. And tagging along might be Phil Hogan, the former Hull KR star loose forward, who lives just down the coast in Barrow.

Do they discuss the merits of nuclear power? It's just the old days when a shoulder pad was something worn by Joan Collins.

Keith Bridges

Age: 55.
Born: Featherstone.
Clubs: Featherstone Rovers, Hull FC and Bradford Northern
Position: Hooker.
Playing era: 1968 – 1983
Double retirement: When Keith - his first name is really John - finished his career with Hull FC in the 1982 Challenge Cup Final and replay he decided to retire from playing.
But he came back? He had an appeal from his former Featherstone Rovers coach Peter Fox who by 1983 was coach at Bradford Northern. Northern's front line hooker Brian Noble was out injured and his normal replacement Tiger Handforth was on under-21 duty in France.

So he was like Eric Prescott's dentist? He filled a few gaps? Yes, but that last hurrah was enough for him and he moved to work in the public house industry.
Highlights: The best moments of Keith's career were playing at Wembley for Featherstone Rovers in 1973 and being selected for the 1974 Great Britain touring team.
Work: Keith, like virtually everybody else in Featherstone worked at Ackton Hall colliery. When it closed, following the miners' strike of 1984, he moved to Sharlston Colliery. But then he moved out of mining altogether and into the drinking trade.
It's still the same business...mine's a pint. 'Mine's' geddit! Keith was a dutiful landlord.
Where were his watering holes? First he had a pub in Rothwell near Leeds and then he worked for eleven years at the Star and Garter pub at Kirkby Overblow near Follyfoot in Harrogate, North Yorkshire.
That's Leeds United footballer Eddie Gray's local: It wasn't a bolt hole for many ex-players.
And today? He's working as one of the staff in Dewsbury Golf Club's clubhouse.

Ian Brooke

Age: 64
Born: Plymouth, Devon.
Father's occupation: Royal Marine.
Clubs: Wakefield Trinity, Bradford Northern
Era: 1961 – 1970
Position: Centre.
First on the list: Ian holds the distinctive record of being the first player Bradford Northern signed in their 1964 revival.
I remember it well: They paid Wakefield £8,000 for his services.
Reason for retirement: Injury - achilles tendon.
Management: Bradford Colts then Wakefield Trinity from January 1978 to January 1979. He was also had coaching stints at Huddersfield and Doncaster.
Earning a living: Ian was a gas fitter and central heating engineer all his working life until retired last year and is now a gentleman of leisure.
For this interview did he say he would be there at 9am and then arrive four hours late and charge you a call out rate? We spoke over the phone.
Shopping: His kids like sport. *"When my wife and I went to the supermarket there was soccer kit and a ball, two rugby balls, golf clubs and cricket gear all belonging to my Grandson, Ben, in the boot. There was no room for the shopping which had to go on the back seat!"*
Highlight: The best moments of his rugby career came when he played in the 1963 Challenge Cup at Wembley and scored a try when he was just 19 years old.
Cool: It was the very last try of the game in the final minute of the game as Trinity beat Wigan 25-10.
Anything else? And he was selected for the 1966 Great Britain tour of Australia and New Zealand playing one of the Tests against Australia at Sydney Cricket ground.
Where seen today? Wakefield Trinity Wildcats' home games in the Super League.

Chris Burton

Age: 50
Clubs: Leeds, Huddersfield, Hull KR, Featherstone Rovers
Playing era: 1974 – 1995
Reputation: If you ask any Australian who was knocking around Rugby League in the 1980s about Chris Burton, be prepared to take cover. Chris didn't take many prisoners and the Aussies didn't like him one bit.

Calling it a day: Chris followed the trend of the era and left his retirement late. *"I was knocking on a bit when I decided I was getting to slow for it all. I was 38 years old."*

Hot wire: When he was playing, Chris was an electrician. He then got a job as a service engineer and that's what he's doing for a living today.

Coaching: After he retired as a player Chris went into coaching. He went to work at Featherstone Rovers with Kevin Hobbs whom he'd met during his time at Post Office Road - or the RJB Stadium - or even the Chris Moyles Stadium.

And today: Chris is enjoying himself passing on his knowledge and love of Rugby League working in the Leeds Service Area and with Leeds Rhinos' Scholarship Scheme.

Staying in touch: Chris is one of the quiet men of Rugby but he also enjoys the company of men who have been good players during their careers. He's a great attendee of re-union dinners and he's been to the ones staged for all of his old club sides as well as those staged by the British Lions Association.

Highlights: The top moments in Chris's career were an appearance in a Challenge Cup Final for Hull KR in 1981 and taking part on the Great Britain tour of Papua New Guinea, Australia and New Zealand in 1984.

Disappointment: He might have made a second Challenge Cup Final in 1986 but for injury. Hull KR fought their way back into the semi-final to earn a 24-24 draw with Leeds and a replay. But when Rovers were beating Leeds 17-0 at the second attempt, Chris was in the operating theatre under the surgeon's knife having a plate inserted into a broken arm!

Len Casey

Age: 54.
Born: Hull.
Era: 1968 – 1984.
Nickname: Iron Man.
Clubs: Hull KR, Hull FC, Wakefield Trinity and Bradford Northern.
Retired: 1989

Was he a respected player? He was a great back row forward and when he moved between the two Hull clubs nobody gave him any stick for changing sides.

The pub trade: Len and his missus, Sue, were publicans in various parts of Hull and there was never much trouble at his gaffs come closing time.

Coaching: He was a player-coach with Wakefield Trinity and then moved to Hull FC as coach. He lasted 18-months at the Boulevard and followed that up with five good years as Beverley amateur club coach, taking them through to play in the Challenge Cup against professional club Batley. No other clubs were prepared to take him on because directors would have been too scared to sack him!

Why did he retire as a player? When he was player/coach at Wakefield they played one wet Sunday afternoon at Whitehaven. *"I was soaking, there was mud everywhere; I'd just had a bit of a 'do' with Peter Gorley and I thought to myself – I'm out of here."*

New job: He moved to the Lake District where he now runs a successful bed and breakfast business.

Family life: Len and Sue's have one grown-up son but he's turned his back on the B&B business.

Rugby Leeeeeague: Len still gets down to Humberside ex-players functions and enjoys a few jars with his mate Eddie Bowman, the former Wigan and Great Britain forward.

What does he remember about turning professional? Len's always been shrewd when it comes to cash. When he was thinking of turning pro in the '60s he knew that Hull FC didn't have much cash. When Hull KR's directors turned up at his house in a Roller and a £6,000 cheque his mind was made up.

Dave Chisnall

DOB: 10 April 1948.
Born: St Helens
Clubs: Leigh (twice), Warrington (twice), Swinton, St Helens, Barrow.
Playing era: 1967 – 1987
Position: Prop forward
Game plan: Push, then push harder.
Retirement: It's difficult to pin down when Dave actually retired. He made more comebacks than Frank Sinatra.
Go on, I'm listening: When he was assistant coach at Leigh, St Helens and Warrington, he would pull his boots on again

and again and again when they were short of players.
Working life: Today Dave's a fork lift truck driver at Whiston Hospital.

I knew obesity was a problem but isn't there a better way to get patients into bed? *"In my playing days it was difficult to find a job with good money because you kept needing time off to play."*

I thought rugby was played at the weekend? It was but the game was so hard in those days I just couldn't get out of bed on Monday mornings."

So where did he find work? Dave ended up working for Pilkington's Glass in St Helens. He then swapped working in the glass plant for being steward at their sports and social sites in the town. He stayed in the post until being made redundant and then took several other jobs before getting a start at the hospital.

Rare band of men: Dave reckons the highlight of his career was being selected for the 1970 Great Britain team to tour Australia and New Zealand and beating the Kangaroos in the Test series – the last British team to achieve that feat to date.

At home: Today Dave lives in St Helens and he's an occasional visitor to the modern game but he does stay in touch with the ex-players associations at St Helens and Warrington.

Colin Clarke

Age: 62
Born: Wigan
Clubs: Wigan (naturally), Salford, Oldham, and Leigh.
Position: Hooker
Era: 1963 – 1979
Style: A man of his times. A footballing hooker who took them all on.
Union convert: One of League's most distinctive faces came out of rugby union. He was signed by Wigan from Orrell Rugby Union Club in 1963.
What happened after he finished playing? Colin went into coaching, first as assistant coach

at Leigh, and then in 1982 as first team coach. After Leigh, Colin moved back to Wigan as assistant coach and then as joint first-team coach with former Salford stand-off half Alan McInnes. They were replaced by New Zealander Graham Lowe in 1986 and that was when Colin decided to leave the sport.

Getting his hands dirty: When he was playing for Wigan Colin worked at Leyland Motors as a fitter. He spotted a niche supplying refurbished starter motors, dynamos and water pumps for forklift trucks and set up his own business in 1984. That's where he is today, although competition from the Far East has had a detrimental impact on his business.

You can't compete on price with those Orientals: Why have it repaired when you can buy it new for half the price.

Good luck Colin, still he is nearing retirement age. Will he retire to the Far East? You mean Hull?

Tell me about his family: Two sons - Phil and Andrew.

Justice: Now for a bloke who missed a Challenge Cup Final after being suspended for being sent off, Colin's done well. For the last 12 years he's been a serving member of the RFL's Disciplinary Committee Panel.

He should know all about serving justice then: Colin's wife Margaret had years of being introduced as 'Colin's missus'. Now she's introduced as 'Phil Clarke's mum' after their son became one of the faces of the sport on Sky Sports.

Phil Clarke

DOB: 16 May 1971
Born: Wigan
Playing era: 1988 – 1997
Clubs: Wigan, Eastern Suburbs
Position: Second row forward
Trademark: Scrum cap.

Sounds like a type of poisonous mushroom: It is what he wore to stop his ears looking like a bag full of Cumberland sausages.

How did he get in to the game? His father Colin Clarke both coached and played for Wigan.

The back door you mean? No, he still had to earn his place and he was a talented player.

Most likely to be seen in the flesh: West London on his way to Sky Sports studios.

Lives: Wigan.

Bad break: Phil's career came to a shuddering halt at the age of 24 after doctors told him never to play Rugby League again after suffering a serious neck injury playing in Australia.

Don't tell me, he turned up at Leeds: He took doctors' advice and quit.

Educated: Phil studied Sports Science at Liverpool University.

Work: While he was playing with Wigan he, together with his brother Andrew, set up a sports consultancy business called 'Healthworks'. They provide fitness programmes and advise businesses about health and fitness awareness. The business also involves an element of personal management for professional rugby players.

Selling them pensions and doing contracts you mean? Much more than that. Phil became one of the sports youngest ever senior administrators when he was appointed as chief executive at Wigan Warriors but he didn't stay in the post long, leaving after a year.

And then? He was appointed as team manager for Great Britain in 2001 but stood down in 2006 after becoming disappointed with the British game's international progress.

On the box: Phil has become an important member of the Sky Sports commentary team.

Terry Clawson

DOB: 1940.
Clubs: Featherstone Rovers (twice), Bradford Northern, Hull KR, Leeds, Oldham, Wakefield Trinity, Hull, Newcastle (Australia)
Position: Forward
Playing era: 1957 – 1980.
That means he finished playing when he was 40: Too right.
Reputation: TC was known as one of the funniest men in the game.
Give us an example: Well...how many rugby league players does it take to change a

light bulb? One less than it would in rugby union.
He should get all that written down in a book: Terry actually already spilled the beans on himself in a book called 'All the Wrong Moves'.
Power to the people: Terry was a fitter by trade who worked on power stations and he did that throughout his whole working life.
He was the national grid: Terry was often sent to work on power stations all over the country and that often involved some interesting journeys back for training sessions.
How can a journey back to training be interesting? Did he do it by horseback? It was in the days before motorways and speed cameras, if you get my drift.
Fighting back: Terry had to lose a complete year out of playing the game in 1963 when he was diagnosed with TB. He had six months in hospital before he emerged and started his comeback. He fought his way back to fitness and returned to Featherstone Rovers but he was transferred to Bradford Northern after falling out with the Post Office Road club. Mind you Terry didn't stay that long.
Sport: Terry's a big horse racing fan. He tried golf but didn't like it.
Maybe polo is more his bag: Perhaps.
What's his carbon footprint? Size 10.

Gary Connolly

DOB: 22 June 1971
Born: St Helens.
Who would play him in his Hollywood movie? Matt Damon.
Clubs: St Helens, Wigan (twice), Leeds Rhinos, Widnes Vikings.
Part of: The RL brat pack of the early '90s.
Retired: 2004.
Where seen: Full back or over your try line.
Lives: Wigan.
Emerald Isle: Gary finished his playing career by playing rugby union for Munster in Ireland.

That's like Gordon Brown joining the BNP party. There should be a law against it: During his RL days he played union for Harlequins and Orrell so we still saw him in action.
How did he find the Irish? *"They were wonderful people. Very flexible about my contract, allowing me to go back to the UK frequently to be with my family who had stayed in England."*
Join the crew: Gary was a joiner. He worked for his uncle and had one day a week at college. But all that came to a stop when he was selected for the 1992 tour of Papua New Guinea, Australia and New Zealand, when he knew he was going to be away from the UK for three months.
Building a new trade: Gary has returned to the building trade and is about to take a more 'hands on' approach to the business now that he's finished with rugby.
Gary the grafter: Gary's shares a business partnership with former Wigan and Great Britain captain Andrew Farrell and during 2007 they converted a former nursing home in nearby Standish into a block of 11 apartments.
A haven for ex-players in years to come: Gary has a close friendship with his next door neighbour - former Wigan club mate Kris Radlinski.
Squashing more in: His main sporting focus is squash and plays two or three games a week but couldn't beat Ellery Hanley just yet.

Gerald Cordle

Age: 46
Born: Cardiff.
Club: Bradford Northern
Playing era: 1989 – 1996
Position: Winger.
Fans' nickname: Teflon.
Pre-League career: Before Gerald left Welsh Rugby Union to come north, he was employed by the council in Cardiff in their building construction department. He was tapped up for Northern by another of their major Welsh signings, Terry Holmes.
And after league? He went back to work for the Council but

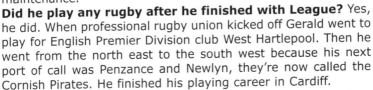

this time in the highways department working on road maintenance.
Did he play any rugby after he finished with League? Yes, he did. When professional rugby union kicked off Gerald went to play for English Premier Division club West Hartlepool. Then he went from the north east to the south west because his next port of call was Penzance and Newlyn, they're now called the Cornish Pirates. He finished his playing career in Cardiff.
New sports career: For a bit of a laugh he went into non-league soccer in South Wales and he played for a club in the Barry League. He switched between striker and playing in goal. And when that got too much for him he took over as the club's manager.
Did they do anything? Yes, they did because they won the league and cup before stepping down.
What does he do with his time now? Watches his son play for Barry RUFC.
Mates: Gerald still sees some of his old League mates who live in Wales, including Phil Ford of Warrington, Wigan, Bradford, Leeds, Wales and Great Britain fame and the amazing David Bishop who tried League with Hull KR.
Highlights: Playing for Wales at league and being part of the Welsh team who played in the classic 1995 World Cup match against Western Samoa in Swansea.

Kel Coslett

Age: Where's my bus pass?
Clubs: St Helens, Rochdale Hornets.
Playing era: 1962 – 1977
Retirement: Like so many other personalities in league, Kel's first decision to finish with the game was overtaken by events. After playing 500 plus games for Saints, Kel decided his playing days were over and he started work as assistant coach to Eric Ashton at Knowsley Road.

Then what happened? Rochdale were looking for a new coach and they persuaded Kel to find his boots and start as their player/coach. He had one year in the job and, finally, his playing career was brought to an abrupt halt by injury. He fractured his knee cap in three places playing against Bradford Northern and after surgery he was left with just half a knee cap. He finished playing at the age of 37.

Working life: During his playing career Kel had several jobs. He was a drayman with a brewery and then he had his own haulage business with a tipper lorry. Then he found a lasting career in brewing when he became a representative with the old Whitbread brewery.

So he left RL behind? After 15 years supping, Kel returned to Rugby League management when he became the Rugby Manager at St Helens. He looked after team logistics thus freeing the coach to concentrate on tactical matters and player preparation.

Did he analyse stuff on computers a bit like Sir Clive Woodward and then put them into spreadsheets to give to coaches as powerpoint presentations? No.

So what does he do now? Kel is St Helens' Match Day Manager. His responsibilities involve making sure everything the team needs is delivered when required. We're talking off the pitch, not on it.

I guess that's where his experience of the brewery comes in? The game's not like that anymore. It's mineral water these days.

Andy Currier

Age: 41.
Unique: One of the tallest men ever to play rugby league - 6ft 6".
Born: Widnes.
Clubs: Widnes, Featherstone Rovers, Warrington, Workington Town
Playing era: 1982 – 2000.
Pioneer: Although Andy didn't retire as a rugby player until 2000 his League career actually ended in 1996. He was one of the first League stars to be tempted into the lucrative world of Rugby Union.

He set the mould? After he had finished at Workington Town he was signed up by London Welsh and then Worcester Rugby Union Clubs, extending his playing career by a further four and half years.

Why did he retire? Andy says that the decision was forced upon him because in his last season he couldn't shake off the injuries any more. *"I seemed to break something else every time I played."* AKA The Kit-Kat man.

Then what happened? Like so many other boys from Widnes, he headed back to the Costa del Mersey and started to drive a taxi in the town.

Isn't it a cab? No it isn't. That's posh London talk. Where Andy comes from it is definitely a TAXI.

Has he had Eddie Hemmings in the back of his taxi? No, but six years on he's still driving the cab. He can't avoid the Widnes club and rugby league though, because so many of his passengers still recognise him from his playing days.

Does he like his new career? It gives him the spare time he needs to spend time with his family and play golf.

What's his handicap? Coming from Widnes – no, just joking. He's a 14-handicapper and like so many other people from the world of rugby league in the region, he's a member of Widnes Golf Club, which means he has plenty of friends when it comes to the 19th hole.

Plans for the future: He plans to make a comeback at the Halton Stadium - as a season ticket holder!

Lee Crooks

DOB: 18 September 1963.
Born: Hull
Clubs: Hull, Leeds, Castleford.
Era: 1979 - 1997
Game style: Always in the thick of it.
Retired: The knees eventually refused to take another step forward on a professional rugby pitch

Painting the town: When Lee signed for Hull as a 16 year old one of the conditions was they find him a job. The coach at the time was Arthur Bunting who had a painting and decorating business so Lee went to join him. Young Crooks did a three year apprenticeship and emerged as a qualified painter and decorator.

That's a long time to serve? Another four years and he could have become a surgeon: In his own way he was like a surgeon such was the attention to detail when doing some intricate cornices.

During his career: Lee appeared in four Challenge Cup Finals including the famous 1982 replay at Elland Road when Hull beat Widnes.

GB Caps: 19.

Mistakes: *"Looking back at my career I didn't make the most of my time at Headingley. But I was a young lad who had supported Hull all my life and didn't want to leave the club. I was put in position where I had to go so I didn't approach my life at Leeds too well."*

Lives: Castleford.

Back to work: When Lee retired as a player he found a job working as a business development manager for a private pub company. He stayed with them for 12 months.

Then what happened? He went back into Rugby League as coach of Keighley Cougars and he was in charge at Cougar Park from March 1998 until April 1999. Then after a short break he went to be coach at York.

What's he doing today? Talent Identification Manager for the Rugby League. He is responsible for the talent recognition programmes in the RFL's development systems.

John Dalgreen

Age: 52
Born: Batley
Clubs: Halifax (twice), Warrington, Fulham
Playing era: 1974 – 1985
Position: Hooker
Style: Combative.

Work: John worked in the construction industry through his working life. Until two years ago he owned his own building company but the legacy of his professional career meant that he had to sell the business.

What do you mean? He wasn't up to it. Injuries and the like.

What sort of injuries? These days a builder can't work if he can't get a copy of the Sun or a tune his radio into Radio One: During the last few years John has had tremendous problems with his ankles. Although that curtailed his work on the building site, he now has a job with a building supplies company.

A desk job? To add to John's problems, he's recently had to undergo surgery on his hands and wrists.

Home: John lives in the West Yorkshire town of Batley where he devotes his time to his family. He has three grandsons and at least one of them is showing signs of being a promising soccer player.

Tying the knot: John's always been committed to his family and he got married when he was 17 years old.

No connection: Having put his boots away for the last time, John didn't have anything more to do with the game, although his injuries were a constant reminder of what the game can bequeath.

A quote on the modern era: *"I don't see players like the Alex Murphy's, and Malcolm Reilly's who had all the skills."*

Career highlights: Playing for Great Britain in 1982 against an all-conquering Australian team as well as winning a John Player Trophy with Warrington.

Jonathan Davies MBE

Age: Still only 44.
AKA: The Peter Pan of Rugby.
Born: Trimsaran, Wales
Clubs: Widnes, Warrington, Canterbury Bulldogs, North Queensland Cowboys
Playing era: 1988 – 1996
If this was made into a Hollywood Blockbuster: Poor Welsh lad, bags of talent, leaves his country make it big in Rugby League.
Retirement: 1997.
Planning: He courted the media and that paid dividends once he hung up his boots for the last time.

Media Man: Now Jonathan can be seen for most the year on national and regional television where he is a full-time rugby pundit. In fact he's unique because the BBC employs him to talk about both league and union..

Bi-lingual: Jonathan offers the media in Wales an extra option because he is bi-lingual. He speaks Welsh as well as English and that has seen him host his own rugby-orientated chat-show called 'Jonathan' on the Welsh language television station S4C. It is shown on the eve of every Welsh international match.

Pre-league career: Before Jonathan turned professional with Widnes in 1988 he had several different jobs. He started his working life as an apprentice painter and decorator and just before he came north he worked for a finance company in Wales.

Greatest moment: In 1997 he jumped into the sea to save a young girl from drowning.

Holidays: Despite his wealth he always holidays on the Gower 'Riviera' in South Wales.

And when he isn't saving lives? Besides his broadcasting he also works for a management consultancy as a motivational speaker. Among the subjects he addresses in his talks are: 'Handling Pressure', 'Instinct and Genius', 'Teamwork' and 'Attitude'.

Family connection: His brother-in-law is Phil Davies, the former coach of Leeds Tykes union team and current head coach at Llanelli Scarlets union side in Wales.

John Devereux

Age: 41.
Born: Bridgend.
Clubs: Widnes, Bridgend Blue Bulls.
Retired: 2006.
How long was his League career? His league career really ended like so many other recruits from Welsh Rugby Union in the late 1980s when Union went professional and he went home to South Wales.
A sad loss to the game: Devs came back to the game on a part-time basis when the Welsh Rugby League Taffia sanctioned a Bridgend RL team.

Successful again: During that time the Blue Bulls, who also included former League legends Kevin Ellis and Allan Bateman, were very difficult to beat.
Union gap: John filled in his summers by playing with the Blue Bulls. He was also a contracted player with Maesteg Rugby Union Club in the South Wales Valleys. He was what you would call a bi-effectual (good at playing both codes).
Time, Gentlemen please: Eventually Old Father Time caught up with him. He had a cartilage operation and at the age of 40 that was that.
So he's finished with the game? Not at all. He's a media pundit with the BBC in Cardiff and part of their match reporting team.
Business life: The broadcasting is only a part-time interest for John because his day job is as a representative for a major chemical company. His client base are doctors, clinics and nurses, which is appropriate considering how many injuries he had as a player and his reputation for being injury prone away from the playing area.
Entrepreneur: Besides his day job, John's also establishing a corporate entertaining business that focuses on taking company parties to major sporting events as well as organising team building days and conferences.
League or union? League.

Kevin Dick

Age: 50
Born: Leeds (just 500 yards from Headingley Carnegie Stadium)
Clubs: Leeds, Hull FC, Halifax, Huddersfield
Retired: 1992.
Position: Scrum half.
Style: Packed a lot of aggression, skill and drive into a small frame. A moustache to die for.
Genetic: His dad was a loose forward with Leeds in an earlier era.
Child prodigy: Kevin signed for the Headingley club when he was 16.

Personal touch: Leeds were worried Kevin would burn himself out playing too much amateur stuff, so the club's coach at the time collared him outside the Leeds Supporters Club at Headingley and gave him a personal cheque of £2,000 to sign for Leeds. He then had to persuade the Leeds Board of Directors to reimburse him.

On top of the world: Kevin's always worked in the construction industry and in 1983 he, together with his mate Shaun Miller, went into business as roofers and they're still trading today.

Retirement: *"For the last three years I was playing on one leg and surviving on my reputation."*

Coaching: Kevin had interest, from a couple of big name clubs, but he didn't take them up even when amateur clubs asked him to join them. He did a bit to help David Ward and John Holmes when they were in charge at Headingley, but nothing since.

Sport: Golf.

Thinking back: In 1977 he missed out on the Lance Todd Trophy, when his team-mate Steve Pitchford was named as Man of the Match by the media at the Challenge Cup Final even though Kevin had scored a try and kicked three goals as well as a drop goal.

Mates: Whenever there's an ex-Leeds players bash you'll find Kevin and many of his contemporaries. *"We're still thick as thieves."*

Roy Dickinson

DOB: 1957.
Born: Leeds
Clubs: Leeds, Halifax, Bramley and a couple of country clubs in Australia.
Playing era: 1972 – 1992
Position: Prop forward.
Nickname: 'Big Roy' because he was big and his name was Roy.
Did you know? Roy reckons he holds a league record for being the last player to sign for a professional club at the age of 15. Soon after the RFL introduced the 17 year old minimum age barrier.

Give us a laugh, Big Roy: *"We played under assumed names for country clubs in Australia. It was just a working holiday for us and good fun."*

Work: Roy's an asphalter but he's done plenty of different things in his time. For a while after he finished playing he went to work with former Bramley forward Peter Jarvis in the pub and hotel game. Then he ran the social clubs at Bramley and Stanningley. Today he's a Heavy Goods Vehicle Driver.

Going to the game: *"Unfortunately, Leeds Rhinos tend to play on Friday nights and I can't get back to Leeds in time to go. But when I do, I enjoy the experience."*

Highlight. The Premiership Final against St Helens at Central Park, Wigan in 1974 rings a bell:. *"The Leeds front row that day was me aged 17, an 18-year-old David Ward and Steve Pitchford who was 19 at the time. We were up against top stars John Mantle, Tony Karalius and John Warlow and I was crapping myself. But we ran away with the game and smashed Saints that day."*

On Aussie hard man Les Boyd: *"We went down for the first scrum and Les said he was going to rip my head off. I asked the referee Billy Thompson if he'd heard what Les had said to me and all he replied was: "Roy, I think he was talking to you not me!"*

Gary Divorty

DOB: 28 January 1966
Born: York
Clubs: Hull FC (twice), Leeds, Halifax, Wakefield Trinity
Era: 1983 – 1998
Game style: Cultured footballer with a turn of speed.

The last hurrah: He was a Wakefield Trinity player at a time when the club experienced a financial crisis and money was hard to come by. So he called time on his career as a player and looked for a new source of income.

Working life: When Gary joined Hull FC he was a coal man,

delivering supplies around York and then he became a heavy goods vehicle driver. Following his move to Leeds he combined his career as a professional player by moving into the club's office and worked for their lottery organisation for three years.

Was he paid in scratch cards? No. When he was transferred to Halifax he went back on the road, this time as a taxi driver and this was followed by a three-year spell as a house husband. He looked after his children while his wife went back to work.

Then? Gary hit the highway returning to his former trade as a heavy goods vehicle driver. After that he completely changed direction by become a personal finance adviser with a major insurance company. Today he is financial consultant with a leading national bank.

Sport: Gary's major sporting interest these days is golf and he has a handicap of 20. He plays at Fulford near his home in York.

That's a good course and the one where Bernard Langer hit a ball out of a tree: *"Our course is big and long but when I go to play on other courses I murder my handicap because I'm so used to having to deal with Fulford."*

Most fulfiling: Gary believes that he has been at his best as a player when he played for Halifax. He played for Great Britain twice and in most of the game's major finals throughout his spell with Hull FC.

Paul Dixon

Age: 44
Born: Huddersfield
Clubs: Huddersfield (twice), Halifax, Leeds, Bradford Northern, Sheffield Eagles
Retired: 1997. He had enough as a player after 15 years.
Surprise decision: When Paul decided to retire as a player it was a major shock because everybody thought he was going to play on for another year. He was in his second spell at Huddersfield and quit after their appearance against Hull in the 1997 Divisional Premiership Final when the Fartowners beat Hull 18-0.

The reason: Paul says that he didn't really discuss his decision to finish as a player with anybody because he had made up his mind to go out at the top and his last game was on one of the biggest stages in world sport, Old Trafford. He was 35 years old when he called it a day.
Disappearing act: After his long professional playing career Paul took a 'gap year' away from the sport.
How did he earn his living? The Dixon family have had a family farm at Blackmoorfoot, near Meltham in the Pennines close to Huddersfield. It's been in their family for 50 years and Paul works with his dad on the farm, even today.
Crafty ex-forward: Paul had a reputation for being a canny player during his career and his 'footwork' skills haven't deserted him. As part of the family business he won a contract to deliver milk to local schools. And there is method in his madness. *"I wasn't brainy enough to become a teacher but I wanted their holidays. And with this contract I don't work weekends and have school holidays, too."*
Did he desert RL? He's helped out at Huddersfield and Halifax, including a two and half year spell as Director of Rugby at The Shay. He's also worked for the RFL as a Performance Analyst along with former supremo David Waite.
Then the money ran out: Now he's spending his time watching the odd game and building a house.

Steve Donlan

DOB: 1954.
Born: Leigh.
Clubs: Leigh, Wigan, Bradford Northern, Springfield, Trafford, Chorley Borough.
Position: Centre.
Playing era: 1978 – 1989
Playing style: Elegant centre with a touch of real pace.

One that got away: After starting his league career at junior school, his grammar school didn't play league, so he went on to join Leigh Rugby Union Club.
Grammar School boy? He was a bright lad and even turned down Salford RL as an 18 year old.
That is bright: He was about to start his accountancy studies and he didn't think he'd have time to do both.
Did he balance his sheet? Six years later, he qualified, he got married and had a young family and got a mortgage so when the chance to turn professional came again he grabbed it.
Salford again? No, Leigh saw him playing Union and offered the contract he needed.
Something to fall back on: Steve went to work for an accountancy practice in Leigh called Hayes and Associates in 1972 and he's still there. Only now he's the senior partner and owns the gaff!
What's his forte? 'Ensuring clients receive that personal touch so often lost in larger organisations'. He does self-assessment, VAT, inheritance...that sort of thing.
Does he spend much time in the kitchen? Why do you ask?
Well, I've got a small business and I need someone to cook my books: Steve plays it straight down the middle just like he did when he was a player.
Record broken: Steve established a new record for consecutive appearances for Leigh of 174 matches and that was only broken in 1984 when he was called up to captain the England team in a meeting with Wales at Ebbw Vale.

Des Drummond

DOB: 17 June 1958
Born: Bolton
Playing era: 1976 - 1992
Clubs: Leigh, Warrington, Western Suburbs (Australia)
Position: Wing
Game Style: A bit lightweight for today's game but very fast.
Where will you see Des today? If you're lucky in Bolton but he keeps a low profile as far as league is concerned.
Martial Plan: Des always had more strings to his sporting bow having arrived in the game as a black belt at judo.

He reminds me of one of the

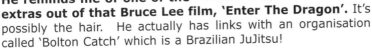

extras out of that Bruce Lee film, 'Enter The Dragon'. It's possibly the hair. He actually has links with an organisation called 'Bolton Catch' which is a Brazilian JuJitsu!

A bit like Samba? Kind of.

Superstar: During the 1980s Des took part in the TV International Superstars competition – the television multi-sports tournament - and in 1982 he set the International Super Stars record for the 100 metres of 10.85 seconds when the event was staged in Hong Kong.

That's where they filmed 'Enter The Dragon'. The only thing he acted on after rugby were the orders of his regulars because for a short time Des ran a pub in Manchester district of Moss Side but left the business after the pub suffered a serious fire.

Not the first time he'd been in the wrong place at the wrong time: What do you mean?

Well didn't he get rendered obsolete with the arrival of the Aussies? I guess you could say they did bring a new dimension to wing play which left Dessie a bit of a dinosaur.

Becoming a star by accident: He'd gone to watch his brother Alva playing in a second team game for Leigh but because Leigh were short of players Des was pressed into service as a makeshift winger. The rest, as they say, is history. He scored 19 tries for the club in his first senior team season.

Ray Dutton

Age: 62.
Born: Runcorn, Cheshire.
Clubs: Widnes, Whitehaven.
An era ends: 1981
Position: Full-back.
Game style: The rock of Gibraltar with the pace to burn.

Cup kings: Ray was one of the Widnes great Challenge Cup fighting team of the 1970s and he was good enough to be one of the players who went on the 1970 tour to Australia and New Zealand.

Late starter: Although Ray had played league from being at school he was not picked up by Widnes until he was 20, when he was playing for now defunct amateur club Widnes Rovers.

Doing it in colour: When Ray was playing with Widnes he had a painting and decorating business with his team mate Mal 'Sam' Apsey. And he kept it going when he packed in playing. He would paint lots of houses in Widnes white.

Disaster: At the same time that he had his painting business he went into partnership in a snooker hall business but unfortunately it got snookered, taking both businesses down. It cost him his house, too.

Not a contender for a job with Alan Sugar then? At least he gave it a go.

Back on top: But Ray fought his way back and now he works as a volunteer driver with the ambulance service in Halton as a car driver taking people to and from appointments.

Bowling along: Today Ray's into crown green bowls. He plays for Moorfields 'B' in the Widnes League. He also does a bit of bowling instructing teaching kids of all ages to play including his own grand-daughter and grandson.

Sporting life: He's also a keen darts and dominoes player.

Guess how his career ended as a player? Running along the beach in St Brelade's Bay in Jersey where he suffered a knee injury.

Joke: He's played with a Kitchin and a Larder for Whitehaven. That's Phil Kitchin and Phil Larder, who later became defensive coach to England's World Cup winning rugby union team.

Les Dyl

DOB: 1953, Castleford.
Clubs: Leeds, Bramley.
Position: Centre.
Playing era: 1968 – 1986.

Couldn't stay away: Les finished playing with Leeds in 1982 and headed out to live in Spain. But when he returned to the UK in 1986 he was tempted back into playing league again with Bramley.

He should have stayed in Spain: Brammers made him captain, though, and he played 22 games for them.

Did he insist on having an afternoon siesta? I don't think coach Tony Fisher would have liked that but he had a style that Les didn't appreciate.

What happened between leaving Leeds and joining Bramley? Les and his wife bought and ran a bar-restaurant in Benidorm and for a bit of fun he played rugby union for two Spanish clubs. *"My brother Malcolm and I were like Gods for these two clubs, because the direct running skills we'd picked up in League smashed the very flimsy Spanish defenses. We had a ball."*

Did they wear 'kick me quick' hats? Les was a founder member of the rugby union club in Benidorm.

Back to Blighty: Les and family headed back to the UK after selling their Spanish business and they bought a hotel and restaurant in Bridlington, east Yorkshire. And eleven years later they're still there!

Does it have a Spanish feel? He brings a bit of the Costa Brava sunshine to the east coast Riviera. They sometimes have paella on the menu but he hasn't got around to organising any bullfighting yet.

Does he organise rugby league training sessions for guests? They could join in with Bridlington Bulls amateur club - the team he helped form.

Sport: Like so many other league players Les was bitten by the golf bug and his handicap is now a respectable 18.

Paul Eastwood

Age: 40.
Born: Hull
Clubs: Hull FC, Hull KR.
Era: 1985 – 1999.
Retirement: He was starting to build his career away from Rugby League knowing the end was nigh.
Working life: While playing for both the professional clubs in Hull he had started to work for a major plumbing and heating supplies company and he could see plenty of opportunities coming his way.
So that's that then? For six months he crossed to the dark side and played rugby union with Hull Ionians.

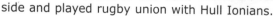

He likes Hull: He also likes golf.
Progress: After he retired as a player he worked his way through the ranks and became manager of the company's operations in Hull. And he must have done well because he was re-located and promoted to manage their branch in Liverpool. Ironically he now lives in the league mad town of St Helens.
Old Trafford: He went to Old Trafford, to watch Hull FC when they faced St Helens in the 2006 engage Super League Grand Final, but he was a long way from the action because he watched the game from one of the hospitality boxes, and Hull lost.
Re-union: Paul was one of the Hull players who gathered together in 2006 to recall their 1980s glory days. *"It was a fantastic occasion when they succeeded in finding and bringing virtually every player in the side that I played with. We had a great day and night out."*
Favourite memories: Paul divides his memories into two bundles. The first is as an international when he played and won against Australia in Melbourne and again at Wembley. And his second bundle is as a club player in the Premiership Final in 1991 when Hull beat Widnes 14-4.

Shaun Edwards OBE

Age: 41
Born: Wigan
Clubs: Wigan, London Broncos, Bradford Bulls
Playing era: Shaun was part of the Wigan Brat Pack who won everything rugby league had to offer in the 90s.
Games: 584.
Wasn't he the guy married to singer Heather Small? You know he was. They never actually married but had a son, James who is ten years old. They're no longer together.
What did he do when he hung his boots up? He was 34

when he retired in 2000 due to injury and kind of went on to be a cappuccino man.
What do you mean? He went to live in London where he was best mates with Martin Offiah.
Capital man: Shaun lives in London full-time these days not just because he's working on the dark side with London Wasps but to be closer to his son.
What about the gong? He picked up an OBE in January 1996 for his services to rugby league. But league is the furthest thing from his mind. He's actually carving out himself as a supremo in union coaching.
Will he come back to League? Who knows? It's a question of whether anybody can afford him and whether it could fit round his family commitments in the south of England. He was reportedly offered the chance of becoming Great Britain Head Coach before Tony Smith was given the job early in 2007 but turned the chance down.
Future: Come on let's be realistic, he will come back to league and be the head coach at Wigan. He might even get the England job in RU since he's doing a great job at Wasps.
Tragedy: Shaun's younger brother sadly died in a car crash in 2003.
Media type: If you want to read what Shaun thinks (and he is a thinker) he has a weekly column in The Guardian but it's about rugby union not rugby league, so probably only good for chip paper.

Keith Elwell

Age: 56
Born: Widnes
Club: Widnes (twice), Barrow
Position: Hooker
Playing era: 1969 – 1985
Stature: One of the smallest men to play in his generation, Keith was a pocket dynamo and he did more than his fair share of tackling.

Nickname: Chiefy. Keith acquired this nickname from his fellow Boy Scouts and it has stuck with him right through his life. He got it for holding a rank with the scout troop.
Durable: Keith established a record of 239 consecutive appearances for Widnes.
And so to civvy street: Through his playing career and beyond Keith worked as a chemical process worker but now he's retired because he suffers from Crohn's Disease. It's an illness that in 80% of patients needs part of the intestines cut away. Recent studies by University College London have found a link between Infammatory Bowel Disease (of which Crohn's is linked) and what you eat. A simple blood test for rasied levels of antibody (IgG) can isolate the protein/blood reactivity and by eliminating the food from the diet, you get better.
Do you mind, I am eating a sandwich: Sorry. Anyway, Keith's best memory was going to Wembley for the first time in 1975 and then playing in the Challenge Cup Final six more times – three victories and three defeats!
Happy days: *"There were some superb guys around like Mick George, Jim Mills, Doug Laughton, Reg Bowden and loads more. It was a wonderful time and I enjoyed it totally."*
Widnes today: Keith doesn't go to the club very often because he didn't like the change from the comfortable old style Naughton Park to the revamped Halton Stadium.
Still a fan: He says that he still wants the club to do well and follows their progress via television and the local media.
Opinionated: *"If you know which side the ball's coming out it's easy to prepare a defensive line. The players look a bit soft to me."*
Lives: Widnes.

Steve Evans

Age: 48.
Born: Featherstone.
Clubs: Featherstone Rovers, Hull FC, Bradford Northern, Sheffield Eagles.
Playing era: 1975 – 1989.

Why did he quit? He promised himself he wouldn't play after he was 30 and when he finished his last game with Sheffield Eagles by helping them to promotion in 1989, it was about a week before his 31st birthday.

True to his word: For ten years, Steve had a sports equipment business in Hull. But he decided he needed a new challenge.

Charity starts at home: Then he went into the financial industry. At first, he concentrated on trying to earn cash as a fund raiser for charities and then he changed tack again.

Sponsorship: In his next guise he didn't earn money. In fact he specialised in giving it away because he became a sponsorship manager with a company called 'Guardian Direct'

Not very rugby league: Another venture took Steve away from Yorkshire to Essex before moving again to work in central London.

The call of Featherstone: Not many league men can stay away from the sport for that long and Steve was no exception. After coming back to West Yorkshire he went back to join his home town and first professional club Featherstone. In fact he was the chairman for a while, and although he stepped down from that office, he is still on their Board of Directors.

Banking on success: Today Steve works for a private bank which has offices in London and Guernsey in the Channel Islands, but he is based from an office at his home in Pontefract.

Specialisation: He specialises in providing financial advice and services for Rugby League professional players. *"I'm trying to provide the lads with the kind of advice I never had when I was playing".*

Coaching: He tried his best with clubs in Norfolk, but Norfolk doesn't play much rugby league, so that didn't go so well.

Richie Eyres

Age: 41
Clubs: Widnes, Leeds, Warrington, Canberra Raiders.
Born: St Helens but he actually is Welsh.
Position: Back row forward

He went on and on: After a glorious League career, Richie extended his playing career by playing professional rugby union for the next five years until 1998.

Where did he go after he finished at Warrington? Well, he had three years playing with Sale Sharks. Full of league rejects.

Famous for: He was one of only a handful of players sent off in a Challenge Cup final (v Wigan 1993).

So when did he hang up his boots? After a year being player coach with Coventry rugby union club. And they wanted him to stay.

Career minded: Even when he was a Leeds player, Richie had an eye on a post rugby career and while the rest of the Leeds team were playing snooker, he toured the building sites in the area looking for work experience as a site manager. And he found it. Before he turned full-time professional as a rugby player, he was a site manager for Redrow Homes after working his way up from being a bricklayer.

Is he still at it? Richie works as a UK national manager for an Irish based steel fabrication company owned by horse racing millionaire J P McManus. That's the guy who used to have a big share holding in Manchester United soccer club. And, yes, Richie does know him!

Does he get to many games? Sadly not. He's all grown up with a family and a construction career to look after.

George Fairbairn

Age: 52.
Appearance: A film extra from 10,000 years BC (the one where Raquel Welch wears a bikini made from a mouse's scrotum).
Born: Peebles, Scotland.
A Scotsman playing RL? Don't sound so surprised.
Clubs: Wigan, Hull KR.
Playing era: 1981 – 1992.
Retired: Aged 36.
What made him stop? Did he keep tripping over his beard? *"When you love the game you just want to keep on going. In the end my body was just knackered."*
And so the end is near: George became the coach of his beloved Hull KR and he stayed working with the Robins for three years. Then he was tempted away and joined Huddersfield as coach for the next two years. And that was the end of it for him.
Ahhhhh: Like so many other players before him George moved into the pub trade and has had some successful pubs in the Hull area.
Where is he today? Co-incidentally George now runs a pub just across the road from where the old Craven Park used to be on Holderness Road in Hull.
How would we know it? Well, it's a converted windmill and by a strange coincidence it's called 'The Mill'.
Does he still have the beard? Oh yes.
Sport: George had a knee replacement two years ago so all he can manage these days is an occasional round of golf and plenty of bike riding. *"The knee operation was a great success and I enjoy the cycling. It keeps me fit."*
Rugby League: George follows the sport on television and is a frequent visitor to Craven Park to see Hull KR in action.
Does he do any jobs in the game? Yes, he does because he's now one of those brave people who serve on the RFL's Disciplinary Committee,
How did that happen? *"I got a letter from the RFL asking me if I was interested in working with them and I jumped at the chance."*

Karl Fairbank

Age: 44
Born: Halifax
Club: Bradford Northern/ Bulls
Playing era: 1986 - 1997
Position: Back row forward
Game style: Bullish and keen with it.
Late starter: He was 23 years old when he started getting paid for playing.
Retired: Aged 34.
And now? Karl works on the family dairy farm at Greetland high up on the moors above Halifax.

Tough business at the moment what with ASDA squeezing their margins. Farming has been a way of life for him and even in his playing days he is still milking.

What are the hours like? *"In my playing days I would get up at five in the morning, milk the cows and then go training. Once I had completed the work out, then it was back to the farm and more work. But I did enjoy it."*

Did he ever have to rugby tackle an errant animal? Only on the pitch.

What about his relationship with rugby? He'd had a bit of success coaching an amateur team when another farmer, Paul Dixon, offered Karl the opportunity to return to the professional game at Halifax.

Today: Karl became the Halifax club's under-21 team coach and is providing the young players the club needs as it mounts its challenge to be restored to Super League.

Highlights: Karl was proud to be selected for Great Britain teams that went overseas in 1988, 1990 and 1992 and won one Yorkshire Cup winners' medal.

Unique: When Karl retired, clubs had started the squad numbering system instead of playing with jerseys with numbers that matched positions. Karl's jersey was number 21 and it was presented to him when he called it a day. And there's still no other 21 jersey in the Bulls squad, even in 2007. It was Karl's number, so he must have made a big impression.

Vince Farrar

Age: 60
Born: Featherstone
Clubs: Featherstone Rovers, Hull FC, Sheffield Eagles.
Era: 1965 – 1984
Position: Prop forward
Style: Old fashioned prop forward. Had a great pair of hands. You needed a crane to knock him down and planning permission to put him back up again.
Retirement: After being very successful at Hull FC, Vince decided that it was all getting too much and decided to retire in 1981. He then took over as coach with the Jubilee Amateur club in Featherstone and as always happens in junior football, one day he didn't have enough players, so he had to pull on his boots for a further three seasons albeit with Sheffield.

Working life: Vince had two jobs when he was playing. He worked for the local council on the roads and was a shaftman *(a man who shafts)* at Ackton Hall colliery in Featherstone. When Ackton closed after the 1984 Miners' Strike, Vince found a new job in the new super pit in Selby so he moved to live and work near the new mine.
Back to Featherstone: After his wife died Vince moved back to Featherstone to be near his family and friends and is now retired from the coal industry.
Does he have his lungs intact? He looks after himself.
A quality player: He was called up to play for Great Britain against the Australians in 1978. Hull FC had been relegated the previous season and Vince was one of the few players called up for international duties from a Second Division club.
Local boys make good: Vince's top career memories centre on his home village club Featherstone Rovers when they won the league title for the first, and so far, only time in their history in 1976-77.
Sounds like a rags to riches story that Hollywood could do: *"It was an amazing achievement for a community of our size and to make it even more special, most of the players came from in and around the village."*

Keith Fielding

DOB: 8 July 1949
Born: Birmingham
Club: Salford
Playing era: 1973 – 1983
Position: Wing
Strengths: Lightning quick and elusive.
Weakness: Tackling.
Conversion job: Keith was lured away from international union to play league and became part of one the game's most successful club players.
Superstar: Keith lived up to the title of superstar when he won the 1981 British Superstars title – a television show featuring multi-sports disciplines and competed for by a host of star performers from different sports.

Wasn't that where Brian Jacks did a million squat thrusts per minute and where Kevin Keegan crashed his bike? Yes. He also won Challenge of the Champions and finished second in the European version.

I think our league stars would romp home in that now if they did it today, but would the coaches let them enter? You'd have more chance of Hunslet getting to the final of Challenge Cup.

Did Keith have any bad moments? After winning the British title, Keith went to Bermuda to compete in the World Superstars championship. He was robbed in a photo finish with Canadian gridiron football ace Brian Budd and collapsed during the 800 metres track race staged in temperatures of 96 degrees farenheight. But, after being rushed away for ice baths and treatments, he gamely returned to the competition to finish fifth. **Work:** During the time that he was playing for Salford he was a physical education teacher at Marple Hall School near Stockport and for the last 26 years he's been head of PE at Bramhall High School, also near Stockport.

Sporting life: After he'd retired as a professional Rugby League player he returned to rugby union, although at a social level, appearing on odd occasions for Stockport and Manchester clubs veterans' teams. His last game was at the age of 50 when he managed 20 minutes in a game with his son Matthew.

Tony Fisher

Age: 64
Born: Dunvant, Wales
Clubs: Bradford Northern, Leeds, Castleford, Bradford
Era: 1964 – 1979
Fame at last: His ears were used as models for the Wallace and Gromit films.

One of the immortals: Tony was one of the key players in the 1970 Test series Down Under.

Hard man: Let's put it this way, if Tony was playing, all the opposition wanted to know where he was at any given time.

A fierce competitor: He used to give 110%.

How did he end up in Rugby League? Tony was in the RAF and came to the notice of Bradford Northern when he went to training at Odsal with his brother.

He swapped one wing for another? *"They offered me a three game trial but they must have liked what they saw because they offered me terms after just two."*

Reason for retirement: Injury.

Working life: Tony started work as a carpenter-joiner on building sites around West Yorkshire and progressed through the industry until he became a site agent.

No rugby on the horizon? Only of a Union nature so I suppose that doesn't count. He actually coached Otley for a short time.

Surely a talent for league: Yeah, Bramley, Keighley, Doncaster and Dewsbury all paid for his services.

Coaching concluded: His last port of call in Rugby League was as coach at Dewsbury, but he remains bitter about the way it all ended, feeling that the game didn't appreciate his coaching methods.

Terry Flanagan

Age: 46
Born: Oldham
Clubs: Oldham, Swinton
Playing era: 1979 – 1990
Greatest asset: A great football brain and pinpoint passer.
Missed out on: Killer pace.
Reason for retirement: Neck injury.

Oldham rugby dynasty: His dad Bill played with Oldham, his brother Kevin was also with Oldham and Terry's son Mark was signed by Wigan Academy plus his nephew Neil Flanagan played for Oldham.

Making it by degrees: Terry decided he also wanted a career outside the game. That's why he signed up for an electrical engineering degree course at the University of Manchester Science and Technology.

Dual career: Terry went to university in 1982 while he was at the height of his playing career and combined student life and rugby life.

The pay off: In 1993 after working in the electrical industry, Terry took the brave decision to go into a partnership and form a telecommunications company. He and his partners could see what was going to happen and that we'd all have mobile phones!

A genius? You bet. Today his company Mason Communications based in Manchester is worth £50 million and has offices all over the world.

He could buy Oldham with that money: He's not getting carried away just yet and has his feet firmly on the ground.

Loves League: He is chairman of the famous amateur club Saddleworth Rangers which is based in the Pennine village of Greenfield, near, yes you've guessed it - Oldham.

Adam Fogerty

DOB: 6 March 1969.
Born: Oldham.
Clubs: Halifax Blue Sox, St Helens, Warrington.
Playing era: 1990 – 1997.
Position: Second row forward.
Late Starter: Adam made a late start coming into league, being brought up on the Isle of Man.
Good move: When the family moved to Halifax it enabled him to play Rugby League.
Taking it on the chin! Adam had a second sporting career, as a professional boxer. He fought in the heavyweight division and, although he didn't win any titles, his record was impressive with just one defeat in 18 professional fights.
Was he ever on the same bill as Iron Mike? No, but similarly, most of his victories came inside the distance.
Let's get ready to rummmmmble! He made his debut in 1987 when he stopped Carlton Headley in the second round. His last fight was in 1991 when he stopped Tracy Thomas in the third round at Kensington, London.
What about defeats? His only loss was to Paul Lister who beat him on points in 1989. But Adam earned his revenge in October 1990 when he stopped Lister in a promotion in Dewsbury.
Did he ever take his work onto the rugby field? No.
And...action! Did I mention Adam's also an actor.
Does he play the romantic leads? With character names like Bruiser, Scab, Urgo, I'll leave you to decide. He was actually in the film 'Snatch' and in a scene with Brad Pitt.
That's amazing: He has done theatre, films, TV and you can see him in action with Brad Pitt on his website.
I love this guy. Does he have an agent? Check this out. He's got two. One in London and another in America.
My missus prefers the soaps: Well he's been in Coronation Street too. They're the real Oscars for us Northern folk. Can you picture him now at a break in rehearsals, playing touch rugby with Rita Fairclough in the car park.
Home: Adam now lives in Spain.

Mike Ford

Age: 41
Born: Oldham.
Look-alike: Actor, Matt Dillon.
Clubs: Wigan, Leigh, Castleford, Oldham and South Queensland
Era: 1983 – 2001

Convert: Mike's another who's found fame and fortune over on the dark side in rugby union. To be fair nobody in league was prepared to give him a job in 2001 so what's a man to do?

Cross the water: Mike started his rugby union career on his own door step by coaching at Dukinfield rugby union club in Tameside. He stayed with them for three seasons from 1999 and then blazed a trail into Irish rugby.

Triple Crown: Mike joined the Irish national team as defensive coach and is credited with helping them win the 2004 Triple Crown – that means they beat England, Scotland and Wales in the same season!

You don't say: Mike returned to England in September 2004 as defence coach to Saracens.

Second time a Lion: Having earned the right to be called a Great Britain Lion when he toured Papua New Guinea and New Zealand in 1990, he gained recognition as a union Lion when he was appointed as a member of the coaching team to the British and Irish Lions tour of South Africa in 2005.

England expects: In May 2006 he took up a job on Andy Robinson's staff with the England team, unhappy at being switched to defensive coach from Head Coach at Saracens.

Oldham connection: He replaced another product of Oldham, Phil Larder, into the England job. Not bad for a town with a professional RL side, loads of amateur league clubs and just one junior rugby union outfit.

Colin Forsyth

The Forsyth Saga began: 25 June 1947
Born: York
Clubs: Oldham, Featherstone Rovers, York, Bradford Northern, Wakefield Trinity
Playing era: 1964 – 1982
Position: Prop forward
A fan would see: A cultured ball handler who could turn on the power and a fair jolt of speed.
Retirement: He just walked away from Wakefield Trinity in 1982 because he'd had enough.
No injury or bust up with the boss? Afraid not.

Don't tell me he began coaching? He'd gone along to watch one of his sons playing for Heworth and before he knew it he was assistant coach to the second team.
He wasn't fed up with the game, just the playing? He eventually took over as first team coach and the club won the National Conference League and reached the National Cup Final. That was 15 years ago and he's not had any connection with the game since.
Business life: Colin started as a scientific and optical instrument maker. He made microscopes and other similar bits of kit. Then he was a fitter and tuner at a car shock absorber company before being an agent for the Prudential for 23 years! At the same time he had a guest house in York.
Pretty busy then: That's not all. One of Colin's other interests is angling and while he was working in the insurance industry he started to look for a fish farm business. Eventually he developed the business so that besides farming the fish, carp and other coarse fishing species, he offers fishing facilities and also offers clearing services for other similar businesses that are over stocked with fish.
I'm a game man myself: Currently it is up for sale.
Record breaker: He and his son Mark played in the same side that played in a round of the Challenge Cup.

Deryck Fox

Age: 42
Born: Dewsbury
Clubs: Featherstone Rovers, Bradford Northern, Batley and Rochdale Hornets.
Era: 1983 - 1998
Retirement: In the end it was the culmination of 15 years of professional rugby. When the eyes told him where to be and his body couldn't manage to take him there, he gave his boots away.

What preparations for retiring had he made? During his time at Bradford Northern he'd started work for Redland Tiles helping make roofing materials. He went up in the world, quite literally, when he switched jobs from ground level to being a roofer.

And is he still on top of the world? Yes, he's got his own roof maintenance company. *"When I took the decision to form my own company I wanted to cash in on my name as a Rugby League player so I had a van with 'Deryck Fox Roofing' painted on the side."*

And is he doing well? Yes, he is and in fact he's just converted his company into a limited company so he must still be on the up.

Is he still into sport? Not really. Work and family commitments keep him pretty busy.

Any regrets? He found out at the 2007 Bradford Centenary Dinner that he's been entitled to two match tickets at Odsal since he left. His younger daughter Isobel is a real Bulls fan and he will use his tickets to take her to the games.

What were the highlights of his career? Playing in the World Cup Final at Wembley in 1992 and coming back from the 1992 tour of Papua, Australia and New Zealand as captain of the unbeaten mid-week team.

Has he the keys of Bradford yet? Who'd want them? He's a regular attendee at British Lions and Bradford's Past Players dinners and would like to go to more Featherstone Rovers 'do's'.

Neil Fox

Age: He gets a winter fuel allowance, let's leave it at that.
Born: Sharlston near Wakefield
Clubs: Wakefield Trinity (twice), Bradford Northern (twice), Hull KR, Bramley, York and Huddersfield
Playing era: 1956 – 1980
Position: Centre who moved into the forwards when he started player-coaching.
World Record: He holds the world record for the number of points in a career: 6,220 and it's unlikely to be beaten.
Four decades: Neil is one of those rare players who can claim

to have played in four decades. He signed on for Wakefield in 1956 and his last game was in Bradford's second team in 1980.
Highlights: Taking the world record was a special moment for him.
Work: He left school and became an apprentice fitter at Snydale Colliery.
Another miner? He moved to the Sharlston pit and then went to work at Wakefield Power Station. He left the power station in 1963 and set up a bookmakers business.
Quite a jump? He got head-hunted by a Leeds bookmaking business before joining Huddersfield Turf Accountant's, Jack Pearson.
Does he have any tips? Don't work in the bookmaking business. He jacked that in to became a sportswear salesman with Worthington Sports in Bradford and later became a partner that bought out the business.
Does he wear trackie bottoms all day? He can wear what he likes now because he retired in 2000.
Lives: With his wife Molly in Wakefield.

Mick George

Age: 56.
Born: Widnes
Club: Widnes
Playing era: 1970 -1982
Playing style: Covered the ground at pace; enthusiasm in both attack and defence.

On a loser: Mick's career came to an end in a reserve fixture against Whitehaven. Coach Doug Laughton was enforcing a policy of first-team players making their comebacks after injury through the 'A' team.

Wasn't the 'A' team that TV series with Mr T and George Peppard? Which one did Mick play? Wrong 'A' team.

So, was he happy to play? Not really because he and his Widnes club-mate Reg Bowden had a betting shop business together and Saturday afternoons were their busiest days of the week.

Did he have odds on him injuring his knee? No.

Not much of a betting man then? The betting shop project didn't last long and Mick moved into the motor trade opening a garage in Runcorn. And that's where he is today, in partnership with his brother Dave.

Will he fix my big end if I mention Widnes? Only if you pay the going rate.

Sport: His knee injury restricts Mick's participation in most sports but he's a real keen horse racing punter. You'll often see him on courses like Bangor and Haydock Park where he can use his inside knowledge to pick a winner.

Does he get to watch much Rugby League? Mick takes in about five games a season at the Halton Stadium and has been encouraged by the progress the Vikings made in 2007.

Scott Gibbs

Age: 36.
Corrrr, a mere whipper snapper: It's what they feed them with in South Wales. He's got all his own hair and teeth too.
Club: St Helens.
Shirt number: 3
Dubbed: The fastest prop in the world despite being a centre.
Playing era: 1994 – 1996.
Retired: 1996 but went on to play Union until 2004.
Reputation: Gibbo was only in the game for two years but he became proof that Welsh rugby union players could adapt well to the 13-man code.

Did he have a job when he played League? No, Scott was a full-time player and went back to rugby union to be a professional player.
What tempted him back to union? A handbag shop in Bridgend? *"It was a commercial decision, plain and simple".* Money.
Did he ever regret returning to Wales? Not really although when he came back north to play in a benefit match at St Helens for Steve Prescott in Spring 2007, he enjoyed the experience so much that he thought for a moment that he might have finished playing too soon.
Currently: These days he's working for a company of commercial property developers called Liberty Properties in Swansea. He looks pretty much like a city lawyer and his title is Development Manager.
The New Wembley: Not so much for his antics as a league player but a bunch of mad welshmen tried to get a section of the new Wembley named after Scott due to his last minute try when the Taffs beat England in 1999. How does the Scott Gibbs Bridge sound to you?
Sport: Scott's sometimes part of the BBC rugby union match coverage team but, apart from that, its business, business and more business for him.

Henderson Gill

Age: 47.
Born: Huddersfield.
Clubs: Bradford (twice), Huddersfield, Rochdale Hornets, Wigan.
Retired: 1990.
How would I recognise him on the field? If he scored a try he would wind up an invisible lasso above his head as a form of celebration.
Sounds good: He also did some hip shaking dances near the corner flags that caught the imagination of world sport.
It's what the sport needed: He was actually spotted down at Huddersfield playing schoolboy rugby at half time but Bradford won his signature.
Why not Huddersfield? Henderson was quite clear when he signed professional he didn't want to play in his own back yard.
When he was playing what did he do for a living? Henderson comes from a musical background and while he was thrilling the rugby league fans around the world he became a disc jockey.
DJ Gill is in the house? What's his opening tune? Hi-Ho-Silver Lining always gets them going.
What did he do after his playing career came to an end? Henderson went into teaching. He studied IT and went on to become a lecturer a Leeds College. But during 2007 that career was placed on hold following yet another operation on his knees.
Cast your mind back to 1985 and that Challenge Cup final. Ray F takes up the commentary: *"Not sensible play this by Wigan, normally a side would take the ball away from the posts to avoid any goal kicks. Oh, good ball from Kenny, to Stephenson, he's got Gill outside him! Now then, he's got 60 yards to go, can he go round Gary Kemble? Oh, he's beaten him. Oh, as good a try as you'll see. All made, for Henderson Gill, by that beautiful pass from Brett Kenny!"*

Andy Goodway

Age: 45
Born: Castleford.
Clubs: Oldham (twice), Manly (Australia), Wigan, Leeds.
I noticed he played for Manly. Do they have a women's league team? Yeah, they're called Womanly.
Era: 1978 – 1994
Independently minded: He was a player who did things his own way and that sometimes brought him into conflict with the clubs he played for.
Is he another who went into coaching? In 1993 he was assistant to Bob Lindner at

Oldham and then in 1994 he took the top seat at the table. In 1997 he took charge at Paris St Germain which was their final year in les Super League.
The French cannot play rugby league: Maybe so but Goodway returned to Britain and in 1997 was named as the Great Britain Coach until 1999. For the latter part of that period he combined the job with being assistant coach to John Monie at Wigan.
It's all good experience: When Monie left Wigan Goodway took over as Wigan head coach but he was sacked in September 1999. He then embarked on a new career in his native Yorkshire as chairman of the Rugby League Professional Players' Association.
What does the job entail? Goodway worked with one of Great Britain's biggest trade unions, GMB, to establish a department that looked after the welfare of Rugby League players and, at the same time, professional boxers.
He is still there? No, a few years ago he decided to swap sun for rain and emigrated to Australia where he now lives.
As a retired sun worshipper? He has the odd barbie now and then but it is very much a life of leisure.

Parry Gordon

DOB: 17 February 1945.
Sounds Irish: Actually born in Wigan.
Club: Warrington
Era: 1961 – 1981
Position: Scrum half
Game style: One of the best uncapped of his generation.
Why wasn't he capped? That's like saying Colin Montgomerie is the best golfer not to win a major. There were better players around at the time. Today he would walk into the GB team.
Even at 62 years of age? Probably.

Flying high: Parry spent his working life working as a fitter-turner for British Aerospace, but he's now retired. Originally he started work for the company when they made propellers for turbo prop and piston-engined aeroplanes and then he took part in their Nimrod project which was Britain's radar reconnaissance plane. By the end of his time with the company he was working on guided missiles and rocket launchers.
He could have become GB's first and only rugby playing astronaut: When the plant closed down, he took a redundancy package and is now living in retirement in his hometown of Wigan.
Another place with no much atmosphere. Let's chat about coaching: He had several offers to go back into coaching after a three year spell with Warrington but didn't feel he fitted into the coaching mould. It's all manuals and two-day breaks to Lilleshall.
Hobbies: *"I really love watching sport and over the years I've developed a passion for watching golf on TV. In fact if Rugby League and golf clash on TV – golf often wins".*
What else keeps him out of mischief?: Once a week he's off to the river bank where he's learning to be a fly fisherman.

Peter Gorley

Bingo Age: 55.
Born: Great Broughton near Cockermouth, Cumbria
Clubs: Workington Town, St Helens, Whitehaven
Proud: Still has all his own teeth.
Era: Just over a decade until 1986.
Late starter: He wanted to stay amateur for as long as possible because he wanted to play for the GB amateur side.
So what changed his mind? Money and offers.
Who? Workington Town, Salford, Wigan and Leigh all came after him. But he put them off to have some thinking time but the Workington Town chairman Tom Mitchell caught up with him in his village pub and got him to sign.
Pity he didn't have an agent? The only agent in those days was James Bond.
Work: Peter worked in an open cast coal mine where he drove plant and machinery. Today he works in his village of Broughton, for a plumbing company which is owned by Alan Varty, the former Workington back row forward.
Highlights: For Peter playing alongside Mighty Mal Meninga for a spell at Saints.
Hobbies: Fell walking.
That's my hobby too, at times. I had a few drinks the other night and fell walking.

Bobbie Goulding

DOB: 4 February 1972.
Born: Widnes.
Clubs: It would be easier to name the teams he hasn't played for. He's had more clubs than Ian Woosnam.
Playing era: 1988 – 2005
Position: Scrum half & hooker
Game style: Aggressive. Had discipline problems.
Car trouble: He wanted regular first team action and was granted that wish by Doug Laughton. The relationship foundered when there were allegations about dints on Laughton's car. He also had minders to keep him out of mischief when he was on International duty.

He sounds like trouble: All part of what goes in to making a great player. In 1999 he was ordered to do 248 hours of community service for an incident on a stag do in Warrington. Shall we get back to rugby?

Be my guest: When he was given the captaincy of St Helens, he also got a new spelling of his name. Instead of Bobby he became Bobbie.

Coaching: He was player-coach with Rochdale Hornets but quit his post in November 2005 citing frustration with the club's parlous financial position.

Family: Four children and wife Paula is studying to become a teacher.

Lives: Between St Helens and Widnes.

What of the man today? He nearly got a coaching job at Rochdale but talks broke down but then they got going again and he was appointed their coach for a second time in September 2007. Good luck.

Ken Gowers

Age: 71.
My memory doesn't go back that far: He played for Swinton for 20 years until 1973.
Born: Wigan.
Position: Fullback and scrum half.
Game style: Pint-sized defender with pace.
Record-holder: Still holds club record 601 appearances, 970 goals and 2,105 career points.
Car less: He didn't drive, so Ken used to catch the express bus from Rochdale to Manchester, race across the city to Victoria Bus Station in Salford so that he could make his connection to Swinton.
Building on experience: Ken was a qualified bricklayer and he formed a building company in Rochdale. One of the reasons Ken retired as a player was because he'd bought a plot of land in nearby Bury and he wanted to build a house for his growing family. He still lives in it.
Is it finished? The builders I used were useless. They needed a skip just to hold all the sugar they have in their tea. No building regs in Ken's day.
Room mate: On the trip Down Under, Ken roomed with the team's captain Harry Poole from Hunslet.
So he always got a game? It was the next best thing to sleeping with the coaches wife.
Do I know you? Ken and his wife were on holiday in Tenerife a couple of years when Alan Hardisty and his missus walked into the same bar.
It's a small world but so what. I bumped into Bill Murray on a golf course last week: I'm just telling you, that's all.
Happy memories: Ken's still a regular attendee at Swinton ex-players functions and can occasionally be seen at Rochdale's games too.

Jeff Grayshon MBE

Age: 58

Looks like: A bouncer at a Status Quo concert (throwing people in).

Born: Birstall

Kit: He had the biggest chest and the smallest shorts in rugby league history, possibly.

Clubs: Dewsbury, Bradford Northern (twice), Leeds, Featherstone Rovers and Batley.

Playing era: 1968 – 1996

The end: He fell out with Batley where he had been player/coach following the departure of David Ward.

In real life: Jeff is a supervisor at a company involved in the building trade and he is responsible for up to 30 other workers. But he's not been able to work for the last 18 months or so because of health problems.

Playing legacy: Like so many other former Rugby League players Jeff needed to have a knee replacement operation but, unfortunately there were complications and he suffered a stroke. The road to recovery has been long but now he's on the mend. The concern for him is that his other knee now needs replacing.

Royal recognition: In 1992 Jeff was awarded the MBE for his services to rugby and received his award at Buckingham Place from Her Majesty the Queen.

Any regrets?: Jeff was one of those players destined never to reach the Challenge Cup Final at Wembley.

Record breaker: Jeff became the oldest man to play Test rugby for Great Britain at the age of 35 when he was called up to stabilise a shaky British pack. *"The way the game is today I can't see that record ever being beaten".*

Andy Gregory

Age: 46.
Born: Wigan.
Clubs: Widnes, Warrington, Wigan, Leeds, Illawarra Steelers (Australia), Salford.
Era: 1978 – 1995.
How would I recognise him on the pitch? He's the little with his shirt sleeves rolled up to his armpits. It's a style you might see these days on Kate Moss at London Fashion Week.
Retirement: Years of playing at the highest level and drinking Guinness finally caught up with Andy when he was at player coach at Salford in 1995.

Hitting the news: Andy's battle with booze was revealed by the 'Sun' newspaper and later he explained the full extent of his problem in his autobiography that was called 'Pint Size'.
What did the critics say? One summed it up as thus - the story from on-field swagger to the off-field swigger.
Working life: Since Andy retired as a player he's been in and out of the game at various stages. Until autumn 2007 he was the coach with National League Two club Blackpool Gladiators – they didn't win a match while he was in charge although to be fair to him it was a team of players he inherited.
Marital status: Divorced.
What does a recovery booze addict do when he's no longer married? He's runs pubs in Newton-le-Willows in Merseyside and Wigan.
Headlines again: Andy was back in the newspaper headlines in 2007 when he almost lost his life outside a Wigan pub. He had called in after being to a match at Blackpool and tripped over when he came out. Not much problem there you might think but Andy hit his head on a kerbstone as he fell. Such were the extent of his injuries that his life was under threat for a short time, but fortunately this great little rugby league character has staged a complete recovery.
Would he make it in to your dream team? Yes. One of the best scrum halves ever.

Clive Griffiths

Age: 53
Born: South Wales.
Other famous Welsh people: Max Boyce, Vinnie Jones, Aled Jones.
Clubs: St Helens, Salford.
Playing era: 1979 – 1986
Position: Full-back.
Money grabber: He came to league for the spondulicks. But he is one of the few Welsh players who came north and stayed.

He didn't throw it all away and go back to union country? Not as a player. Actually, he was glad he signed for St Helens as it was an opportunity to work at Cowley School.

Retirement: Clive finished as a pro after two years at Salford. He'd been playing with a pelvic injury for quite some time and, after losing his first team place, he decided enough was enough.

Coaching: After a spell out of the game Clive went to work at St Helens as a fitness coach.

A fitness coach with a pelvic injury? It worked okay for him but as assistant coach at Warrington they lost 80-0 at St Helens.

Doh! By this time coaching was in Clive's blood and he moved into pro rugby union with London Welsh then to Swansea and the Welsh national team. He took over at Doncaster before eventually moving to join former Welsh national coach Mike Ruddock at Worcester.

Any skeletons in his cupboard? After finishing as a league player Griffiths was tempted back into second rate union playing under an assumed name.

Which was? 'Chris Griffin'.

You would think he could come up with something more creative like Siggy Popperpopperpoppolis? He didn't want to draw attention to himself, but one opponent did complain about them playing with ex-pros in their fourth team.

Jonathan Griffiths

DOB: 23 August 1964.
Born: Carmarthen, Wales
Club: St Helens.
Era: 1989 – 1996
Position: Scrum half.
Game style: In your face Welshman who had pace a bit like Shirley Bassey.

Putting out the flames of firey situations: Before JG came up to be a full-time Rugby League player he was a fire-fighter. After his rugby playing days were over he picked up his hose pipe again and has returned to the fire and rescue service in West Wales.

There used to be a lot of fires in Wales. I suppose he was kept busy? In the 80s some of the more radical Welsh extremists set fire to holiday homes owned by the English and that kept them busy but he still found time to play rugby with Llanelli and Haverfordwest when he went back.

Did he apply his league skills to the union game? He says it was what kept him playing a such a high level for so long.

What were the top moments in his Rugby League career? Going to Wembley in 1991 topped the list for Jonathan even though Saints were beaten 13-8 by Wigan.

Could he have stayed among the northern flock after league? Yes, Jonathan had a couple of job offers but the call of Wales proved too strong.

Where does he live now? He lives on the coast at Haverfordwest in Pembrokeshire. Interestingly, Pembrokeshire is the only coastline of the UK with National Park status.

What about North Yorkshire with its coastline? You've got Whitby, Hornsea, Flamborough? And Skegness and Cleethorpes.

Point taken. Tell me what he does to keep fit these days? He still plays a bit of cricket. One of his other sporting interests is taking part in triathlons with his mates.

Doesn't he do sedate? He played a bit of golf when he was on Saints books but he can't recall where he put his clubs when he moved back to Wales.

Adrian Hadley

Age: 44
Born: Cardiff
Clubs: Salford, Widnes.
Playing era: 1988 – 2001
Position: Winger
Nickname: Adolf – facially he shares common features with the former German dictator.

Is his wife called Eva? No.
Why did he choose league? He wanted a change of scenery from the dark side of rugby union.
Salford is far from 'scenic'.
Retired from league: 1996.
Then what? He went back to union playing at Sale Sharks. He became director of rugby until a run of bad results meant he was given the full backing of the board in 1999.

That can be painful: His partner got a job working as a fund raiser with Hibernian FC and while she was out earning the 'shekels' he wrote his autobiography.

What was it called? 'Codes of Misconduct'.

Sounds like an expose? It lifted the lid on the pro game.

And could he work again or did he have to get out of town? He took over as chief executive at Bridgend but was made redundant. His next job was as Operational Director for a hospice near Newport, Gwent and that's where he is today.

Two facts about Adrian Hadley: He won a gold medal as an athlete at the Welsh games and was voted as 'the most promising player in Wales' in 1983.

What he thinks about league and union: His comments were actually reported in Parliament.

What did he say, Mr Speaker? League and union are two separate sports with different sized balls.

Steve Hampson

Age: 45
Born: Wigan
Teams he turned up for: Wigan, Halifax, Salford, Widnes, Cannes (France).
Oh la-lah: He didn't learn the lingo though.
Position: Full back.
What's that in French? Le full back.
Retired: 1997.
Then what? He focused on the fitness industry.
So fit he could still play rugby? Not for Sale Sharks he couldn't. They had some great players but he did spend six

years looking after Jason Robinson, Charlie Hodgson and Mark Cueto.
His only job? No, during that same time he worked as a fitness and conditioning coach with Lancashire Cricket Club.
What like Fredelo Flintoff? My Grandmother could beat him over 50 metres. Freddie is deceptively fast - a bit like Glen Lazarus. One of his other clients is former England number three batsman Neil Fairbrother who has used Hampo's methods to 'fit out' the England cricketer team.
Okay, who else? In union he's worked with England wingers Steve Hanley, David Rees and Phil Greening.
I can see a festive DVD coming out: Steve's Christmas Hampo.
So what's he doing now? Well he's come back to where the grass is always greener - league.
Good lad: In May 2007 he was appointed fitness guru to the Great Britain Rugby League team. He's also undertaking a remedial massage course. Massaging a few gums no doubt.

Ellery Hanley

DOB: 27 March 1961.
Born: Leeds.
Left School: 16.
Clubs: Bradford Northern, Wigan, Balmain (twice), Western Suburbs, Leeds
Playing era: 1978 -1997
Legend: One of the best ever players in the game, ever.
Nickname: The Black Pearl.
Nice title for a film too. Who'd play Ellery? Wesley Snipes.
Game style: Electric. He could score from anywhere in a second. Remember that try for Bradford where he ran the

length of the touchline fending off tackles like Steve Irwin would snakes?
Remember it? It was on the opening titles of Grandstand for years. It was Frank Bough's favourite try. Where might I see him today? At the David Lloyd gym, Leeds. He's a man of leisure and one of the first to have made a lot of money from the game. He's still got a house in Australia although he lives over here in Leeds.
Does he use the gym? He's a fierce competitor on the squash court and plays a mean game of chess.
Honours: In 1989 he was awarded the 'Golden Boot' which recognised him as the best player in the world. In January 1990 Ellery was honoured by Her Majesty the Queen when he was awarded the MBE for services to rugby league.
We're not worthy: Ellery was a full time player for most of his career and today has built himself a career away from sport as a property developer. Believe it or not he also officially launched a recruitment business called Penman.
Coaching: His first high profile appointment was as Great Britain coach in 1994.
Wow: In 1999 he was appointed as head coach at St Helens. He also dabbled in union having coached at the Bristol club and with the England national team back room staff.

Alan Hardisty

Age: Here's a clue. He gets a winter fuel allowance.
Guess what, so does Paul McCartney and Rod Stewart.
Born: A former mining town near Leeds called Castleford.
Clubs: Cas, Leeds.
Retired: 1973.
Nickname: Chuck.
Reason for retirement: Wear and tear. But he must have liked retirement because he did it twice.
How come? Well once his former coach Derek Turner heard that he was not with Cas any more so he approached Alan to resume his career at Leeds.

Didn't Alan play in Australia? Yes, he did. He was a player coach for three clubs in Queensland but now puts those three and half years down as a mistake. *"It was too hot for me out there".*
He should have gone to Whitehaven. Anyway, what happened after his rugby career? Alan opened a health centre in Castleford and that ran for ten years.
Having injuries helped build that career? When he was injured during his playing days he went to see Charlie Blackburn, the blind physio, and it was Charlie who first stirred Alan's interests in being a remedial masseur.
And does he still enjoy it? *"I've been quite successful in the field and, although I want to slow down a bit, my clients won't let me because they keep coming back for me to treat them."*
Hobbies: He plays golf religiously on a Sunday.
What in a surplice and cassock? What I mean is he plays every Sunday. He's got a handicap of 16.
Favourite golfer: Tiger Woods.

Paul Harkin

Age: 49
Born: Wakefield.
Clubs: Bradford Northern (twice), Hull KR, Leeds, Halifax, Hunslet.
Playing era: 1973 – 1993
Position: Scrum half.
Status: One of the best half-backs of his generation.
Working life: During his playing career he was a gas fitter but today he's retired. A thrifty Yorkshiremen he invested the money he made and now lives off his pension and investments.

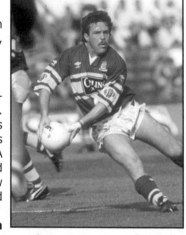

He isn't an investor with Northern Rock then? *"I used to make more money from the game than working so I was always planning for the future."*

Part-time work: Today you'll find Paul in the press boxes around Super League because he works part time as a match reporter for the Press Association. He's one of the former professional players employed by the news agency to go to games and supply them with a running commentary, including all the statistics.

What helped shape him as a player? Brisbane when he was a 26 year old was key. Not just maturing him as a player, but also as a person. He didn't find it too hot either.

Coaching: Paul was called into look after Wakefield Trinity's under 21 team then took over the first team job when Dave Hobbs left. But he was eventually replaced by Australian Peter Tunks.

Representative puzzle: Given his impact on the game during his time, it is surprising to learn that Paul never played for Yorkshire and gained just one Great Britain cap playing in France.

If that was American Football he could have sued their asses: Yes, but it isn't American football, is it.

Neil Harmon

DOB: 9th January 1969. A chilly day in St Helens if I remember rightly.

Clubs: Warrington, Leeds, Huddersfield Giants, Bradford Bulls, Halifax, Hull KR.

Retired: 2002

Position: Prop forward

Moment of truth: When subbed after taking a smack on the chin.

What did he say? *"That's it mate, I've had enough."*

And did he? Yes. He hung up his boots thereafter.

To get a good education behind him: While Neil was playing with Warrington he gained a degree in Electrical Engineering from Manchester University, so it's Neil Harmon BEng (Hons).

Did he think about trying for a job in the game? Why would he do that with all them letters after his name.

Man of Property: During his playing spell with Leeds, Neil took the time to invest for his future by buying a few houses that he rents out.

Switched on: Neil's big business venture right now is a pub in West Yorkshire. He's in partnership with three other guys, including Henry and Robbie Paul but Neil's now the driving force behind the project.

Any Lisa Riley moments? Mid-way through a match for Warrington, Neil was getting warmed up and ready to come on as a substitute and was running up and down the side line. He was so wrapped up in the on-field action that he ran straight into the touch judge who was running the other way. Both of them were out of it for a time and had to receive treatment.

Here's your £250: It wasn't captured on film.

Brendan Hill

Age: 42.
Born: Halifax.
AKA: The Hulk.
Clubs: Leeds, Bradford Northern, Halifax, Keighley, Hunslet.
Retired: 1993.
Appearance: Big lad whose shorts were always three sizes too small. Sumo wrestlers in Japan have posters of Bren on their wall.
Looks like: A butcher.
Working life: Brendan is still a driving force because he works as a Heavy Good Vehicle driver for one of West Yorkshire's

largest demolition and earth moving contractors. His overalls are not as tight as the shorts.
Dishing out the discipline: *"That was the way the game was played in those days and if you didn't look after yourself somebody was certain to take advantage. I didn't want that to happen to me!"*
Union dues: Even though Brendan is inextricably linked with league – some may say he's become a cult hero for those who saw him play – once he had retired from the professional game, he moved into rugby union.
Not our Brendan? Union? Yes, it's true he played for Bradford and Bingley and then moved north to play for Harrogate.
Missed opportunity: Brendan was in the GB team but when it came to his big day to pull on his red, white and blue jersey he had to withdraw from the match suffering with 'man flu' and never got another chance.

Phil Hogan

Age: 53.
Born: Barrow in Furness.
Any relation to the Hulk Hogan? Only in size.
Clubs: Barrow, Hull KR, York
Role: A battering ram.
Era: 1970 – 1990
Peak performer: Phil was a fit lad and wanted the same when he went into coaching at Barrow in 1990. He was recruited as assistant to Steve Norton.
Work: Phil originally worked in the shipyard where he did his time as a fitter. When he went to Hull KR, there wasn't much call for a submarine maintenance attendant, even in a major port like Hull, so he opened his own gymnasium in the east Yorkshire city.
Dual nationality? He left the gym in Hull and took a pub in Barrow. For a while his wife looked after the pub while he commuted to and from Hull three times a week. Finally, the travelling got to him and the pub business went to the wall. Then Steve re-trained as a sports therapist and he started lecturing on the subject at both Barrow and West Cumbria colleges. He also established a sports therapy practice.
Was it tough to make the grade? Phil admits that getting the qualifications was a challenge. He had to get a BTech grade then 'A' levels before he could go to college to study sports therapy. But he triumphed, emerging with a degree.
Well done: He kept his eye in by spending ten years looking after coaching, sports therapy and team affairs for the Furness Rugby Union Club. He finally stepped down from that role in 2007.
Highlights: Phil says that in a 20-year career there were many top moments like winning the Second Division championship with Barrow; four Division One titles with Hull KR; being selected to play for England in the 1977 World Championships; playing in the European Championship against France and Wales in 1978; and playing at Wembley.

Neil Holding

Age: 46.
Born: The Helens.
Clubs: St Helens, Oldham, Rochdale Hornets, Widnes, Bradford Northern.
Playing era: 1977 – 1995
Position: A cheeky chappy scrum half.

Size doesn't matter: Neil's not the biggest bloke ever to play professional Rugby League. For extra cash on a Saturday, he stands on top of wedding cakes. Actually his son is six foot tall.

Working life: When Neil started his working life, he was a chef at a glassworks in St Helens for four years, but after he'd had his second major shoulder operation, he lost that job. Then St Helens took him on to their staff. At first he was selling lottery tickets and then he became a part-time groundsman at Knowsley Road. But Neil had really found his niche and he was soon promoted to head groundsman.

Into soccer: Liverpool FC reserve team played one of their matches at Knowsley Road and were so impressed by the state of the St Helens RLFC pitch that they offered him a job on the strength of that surface. He's now head groundsman at Liverpool FC's training centre at nearby Kirkby.

Show business: Besides being a talented league player, Neil discovered early in his life he was an accomplished mimic and even appeared on kids television programme 'Junior Showtime' doing imitations of late Rugby League Television commentator Eddie Waring.

Wella–er ah, up 'n' under: That extra talent made him a popular member of the Sunday Mirror Rugby League Road Show which toured throughout the 1970s and 1980s raising money for players' testimonials.

Caps: Neil won four caps for Great Britain on the 1984 tour of Australia and New Zealand but never wore the red, white and blue in Britain. None can be worn in cold weather.

Les Holliday

Age: 44.

Born: Whitehaven.

Clubs: Swinton (twice), Halifax, Widnes, Dewsbury.

Moving on: When Les could not meet his own high standards as a player during his second spell with Swinton, he decided to retire.

Working: During his playing career he swapped between engineering and full-time playing.

Coaching: Les had a two-year stint in charge of Swinton Lions stepping down at the end of the 1999 season.

Management: Les's most recent appointment was that of Director of Rugby with Swinton Lions. He spent three years partnering the club's coach Paul Kidd and then at Christmas 2006 he left the club. *"There was a change of direction by the club's management and I decided it was the right time for me to go."*

And today? For the last seven years Les has been working in the battery business and one of the country's major manufacturers who are based in Bolton.

Is it Duracell? Does he work a 25-hour day, 8 days a week, 54 weeks of the year? No.

Family connection: Les is the son of Cumbrian second row forward Bill Holliday, the former Whitehaven, Hull KR, Swinton and Great Britain forward and, as a family, they had a very special day out at Old Trafford, Manchester in 1987.

Historic: That was when Swinton played Hunslet in the first ever Second Division Premiership Final when father Bill shared the Swinton coaching duties with Mike Peers; his younger brother Mike was in the second row for the Lions and Mike played at loose forward.

John Holmes

Age: 55.
I know his brother, Barrett.
Where was he born? Leeds
Club: Leeds.
A one club man? Rarer than an Iranian shooting range in Washington.
Playing era: 1968 – 1990.
That's 22 years! He should be applauded for his effort and his joints: John's not a man of many words off the field but very much a team player on it.
That moustache: For long periods during the 1970s John sported a Mexican style growth on his top lip.

On his RL tombstone: His distribution was better than Eddie Stobart and he could read a game like a book.
Retirement: John called it a day as a player when he was 38 years old.
Did he keep a job within the game? No.
Work: John worked in the printing game for 40 years and is still going strong.
Sport: John's so busy with his family life and work that he doesn't get that much chance to take part in sport these days. He does get some exercise though at his job. *"It's a pretty physical job that I have and it's like going to the gym every day so I'm in good shape."*
League according to John: He's not a lover of the modern style of the game and feels that many of the players with outstanding individual skills are no longer seen.
Dismissals: He was known as a tough but fair player but he had two trips to meet the RFL's Disciplinary Committee. Of note, he was sent off for allegedly dumping his mate John Woods of Leigh on the floor and found himself in trouble with John's wife after the game. *"I never laid a finger on him and when I tackled him about it after the game John just smiled - as you do. I did ask him to put his wife straight on what happened though".*

Terry Holmes

DOB: 10 March 1957.
Born: Cardiff
Club: Bradford Northern.
Playing era: Two seasons.
Retired: 1987.
Not long: He was dogged with injury and only played less than 40 times.
Position: Scrum half.
Value for money: 3 out of 10.
Late starter: He came to league when he was passed his best having had several good years with the Welsh Rugby Union side.
The big switch: Bradford Northern eventually persuaded

him to move codes in December 1985 but the gamble failed for both player and club.
What do you mean? Just 13 minutes into his pro debut at Swinton on 8 December 1985, he suffered a dislocated shoulder and was rushed to the Yorkshire Clinic in Bingley for surgery.
Doh! While making his comeback he dislocated the same shoulder again.
Doh! Doh!: Northern got just 37 games and nine tries for the £80,000 they paid for him.
Nothing to it then, back to the Valleys: It wasn't so simple for Terry. The union boys were still amateurs in those days and couldn't allow Terry back until the game went professional in 1996.
What did he do for brass? His Bradford money was hardly a king's ransom but he got into the demolition business in Cardiff.
Coaching: For two seasons Terry was joint coach of the famous Cardiff Rugby Union Club – the club he had served as a player – from 1996 to 1998, a job he shared with Alex Evans. In the 1998-1999 season Cardiff rebelled over having to play just clubs in Wales and they endured a long-distance fixture list. Terry had the coaching job to himself but he parted company with the club at the end of the season.

Eric Hughes

Age: 57
Clubs: Widnes, St Helens, Rochdale Hornets.
Retired: 1987.
For any particular reason? Broken arm sustained whilst playing for Rochdale. It was his second attempt at hanging up his boots.
Into the pub trade? Actually, Eric was offered the job as coach of Widnes so he took it.
And why wouldn't you? And to remove the temptation of playing again he crossed himself off the playing register.
So why did it all end in tears at Widnes? Because they sold Joe Lydon to Wigan for £100,000 against his wishes and without his knowledge.
Tut-tut: Although finished as a player, Alex Murphy heard that he was no longer on Widnes's books and made him the kind of offer he couldn't refuse.
Which was? To join St Helens as a player.
And what did he do? *"I was one of those rare things in those days; a free agent because I'd crossed myself off the Widnes playing register."*
Civvy Street: Eric used his signing on fee from Widnes to put himself through teacher training college and for a couple of years he worked as a teacher. Then he got itchy feet and set up his own engineering business based near Crewe.
Today: Eric and his partner Jan have a business near Warrington. Eric looks after some accommodation they own while Jan runs her physiotherapy practice and equestrian interests.
Sport: Golf is Eric's new sporting passion. He plays when ever he can especially with his two sons. He's a member at Sandiway Golf Club near Northwich in Cheshire and has a handicap of 16.

David Hulme

Age: 43.
Looks like: A cross between Dean Bell and that Aussie actor out of Strictly Ballroom.
Born: Widnes
Clubs: Widnes, Leeds, Salford.
End of an era: 1998
Seasonal adjustment: Dave was one of the players who spanned the leap from winter league, to the new summer format.
Did he go full-time with the rest? Yes. At the time when the professional era came into league Dave gave up his day job in the electrical trade to concentrate on playing.

What happened when he finished? Well, he was very lucky because he was able to get another job in the same industry. *"I was really fortunate. One of the first interviews I attended after my retirement saw me land a job as a representative for an electrical company in Birmingham. That gave me time to get back on my feet".*
And where is he today? After a year with the company in the West Midlands Dave got an offer to manage the Warrington depot of a company called Cleveland Cables and he took it.
Sackings. Has it ever happened to DH? Don't mention Widnes 2001.
Doh! *"Looking back it was probably a mistake to take the job in the first place. It was just at the time I was settled into my working life and it was a real struggle to work and try to run a Rugby League team at the same time."*
So why did he do it then? *"Well, it was a real temptation to coach my home town club where I'd been so happy as a player."*

Paul Hulme

Age: 41
Born: Widnes
Clubs: Widnes, Warrington
Era: 1982 – 1999.
Faults: Wore a naff headband.
Retired: *"I had a few injury problems, nothing too serious and I've no complaints about finishing when I did."*

What was his day job when he played? He was an electrical engineer. During his playing career he had trained at Manchester Polytechnic and he's still a serious 'sparky' today.

Has he had any shocks? Only when Andy Farrell got in the England Rugby Union team.

What about coaching? He's assisting the Halton Service Area representative teams.

Who are they? Teams put in place by the RFL to ensure the development of the game. Professional clubs, amateur clubs and schools - all working together to produce a definite pathway in the game for players.

What about getting back into the pro game? Paul says he'd love to be involved with Widnes again.

So give it a go, man: He did. When his brother David was first team coach at the Halton Stadium Paul helped out, but swearing on TV programme 'Rugby League Raw' helped get Dave the sack and Paul went with him. If they had a swear box between them they could have bailed out Northern Rock.

He'll never be out of work though if he is a good electrician. Do you know of any other famous electricians? Rowan Atkinson, Michael Faraday, and Dr Frankenstein.

Lee Jackson

Age: 38.
Born: Hull.
Clubs: Hull FC, Sheffield Eagles; South Sydney, Newcastle Knights, Leeds, York City Knights.
Playing era: 1986 - 2005
Why did he retire? Basically he couldn't do the training required any more.

Work: When Lee was playing for York, he worked in the construction industry. He was a licenced operator of a specialised piece of kit which moved bricks and heavy gear around building sites. He describes himself as glorified fork lift truck driver but the equipment he operated had a massive boom and worked high levels.

Is he still in the building game? No, he's not.
What about the forklifts? Now he's working in the sports and leisure industry as a rugby coach and specialised learning aide at Hull College.
What does Lee's work involve? He coaches students in the 'tender' arts of Rugby League and after just a few months working in the Further Education field, he's content.
Any other involvement with rugby league? In 2007 Lee took over as coach to the Hull University team and has had the satisfaction of seeing some of his players go into the professional game with Doncaster and Sheffield Eagles.
Do you think he might become Professor Jackson one day? He's got more chance of joining the Bolshoi Ballet.
Lives: Ferriby.

John Joyner

Age: 52.
Born: Hunslet, Leeds.
Club: Castleford.
A one club man? A servant like you'd never seen before.
Playing era: 1972 – 1992
Age retired: 38. He couldn't keep punishing the body but he didn't leave the club that produced him, because he became assistant coach to Australian Darryl van de Velde and, after Darryl moved on, JJ became the first team coach. But it all ended in tears when John fell out with the club in 1997.

What jobs did he do when he was a player? He had loads of them but one of his first was as a miner. When he came back to the surface he went on to have a fish and chip shop and worked for the club on the fund raising side of the business.

So what does he do today? Well, he has his own courier business and among his main contracts are two wine companies.

Delivering Chateaux Hunslet? John's a bitter man.

Any perks? He gets to listen to Radio One all day in his van.

I got deep vein thrombosis of the ears doing that. What about coaching though? When John left Castleford in 1997 he had an opportunity to coach at Featherstone Rovers but turned it down. Today he helps out with the Upton Amateur Rugby League Club teams and in the 2006 – 07 season they reached two Cup Finals.

Does he fancy a return to the professional game? He admits to having an ambition to go back into action but believes that it might be a bit too late for him.

What were the highlights of his career? Two moments stand out for him. The first was going to Wembley with Castleford in 1986, and being the winning captain when they beat Hull KR 15-14. And the other was when he made his international debut for Great Britain in the second Ashes Test at Bradford in 1978. The Lions even won 18-14.

Chris Joynt

Age: 35
Born: Wigan.
Clubs: Oldham, St Helens
Playing era: 1989 - 2005
Literary aka: The Quiet Man.
Retired: 2005.
Good innings: At a top club like the Saints, you realise it's a young man's game and Chris was no spring chicken.

Regrets? *"If Saints had moved into a new stadium at the time I was coming to the end I might have changed my mind. It would have fired my enthusiasm for another go, but it didn't happen".*

Another union deserter: Only to keep himself in shape and remove some of the aggression. He joined Wigan rugby union club.

Wigan have a Rugby union club? *"I don't play every week and it all depends on my family commitments but I do enjoy it.*

What other sports does he play? Golf.

What about work? Well, Chris on his own admission doesn't do anything at the moment. He's taken a gap year that's spread into two years and may even go into four years.

Sounds like the sort of job i'd like: Chris is still looking for the challenge that will occupy him for the rest of his life. So far he's found nothing that matches up to the challenges he faced in his playing career.

If I asked what his role was in life what would he say? House Husband.

An author: At the end of his career Chris put pen to paper and had an autobiography published called: 'The Quiet Man'. What's not generally known is that the proceeds from this book all went into a Trust which is devoted to helping youngsters from St Helens realise their potential. Not bad for a bloke from Wigan.

Royal connections: Today, he is an ambassador for the Prince's Trust and it has brought him into contact with Royalty as well as attending major award ceremonies.

Tony Karalius

Age: 63.
Born: Widnes.
Clubs: Widnes, St Helens, Wigan, Fulham, Cardiff.
Playing era: 1960 – 1982
Position: Hooker.

On the scrap heap: Tony was a jack of all trades who worked in a scrap metal business in Widnes. He eventually set up on his own.

And?... It is still going. Although he's retired he still finds time to go down to his yard and do some work in the office.

Why would you do that? *"I don't have much to do these days so I like to see what's happening at the yard."*

Has that kept him out of league? He never went back into the professional game once he'd retired as a player at Cardiff.

Any reason? *"I'm not the pushy type and nobody thought it worth while to ask me if I could pass on my experience. I didn't have anything to prove and I never applied for jobs."*

Career highlight: Helping an ageing St Helens beat his home-town club Widnes in the 1976 Challenge Cup final at Wembley when the temperatures at pitch level soared above the 100 degrees farenheight.

Reason for retirement: Injuries.

Staying afloat: Three times a week Tony takes himself off to a local swimming pool and after a short swimming session indulges in a 30-minute running session.

He runs in the water? It might look a bit odd but it takes the weight off his knees. There's actually a Running in the Water Olympics. In four feet of water, the hundred metres record is over five minutes.

Will it be in the next proper Olympics? I doubt it. The pool they use for swimming is eight feet deep, so they would all drown unless each competitor was eight feet and a bit.

Should rugby league be in the Olympics? Aye, along with darts and polo.

Ken Kelly

Age: All the fives. 55.
Born: St Helens.
Clubs: St Helens, Bradford Northern, Warrington, Runcorn Highfield, Oldham.
Playing era: 1968 – 1990.
Work: Before Ken made it to the top of British Rugby League he was a joiner.
It's good to get a trade behind you: Actually his Dad sacked him on the day he got his GB cap because he was playing so much and not working.
Fair enough: A knee injury Ken picked up has had a lasting effect on his life because it was

so serious he has not been able to work since.
Lives: Between Warrington and St Helens.
What, you mean he has two houses and commutes between them? No, he lives in a small town somewhere in the middle.
I suppose he could do the odd bit of joinery here and there: He doesn't have any of his joinery tools any more because they were lost when the old stand at Wilderspool burned down.
Modern game: Today Ken's the hard-working secretary of the Warrington Ex-Players' Association and is the mastermind behind their annual dinner each year.
Highlights: Being picked for two international sides – for the 1972 World Cup in France and the 1979 Tour to Australia and New Zealand. They both figure highly in Ken's memory but he didn't make either trip because of broken jaw injuries. In fact he suffered the second jaw fracture the day before the tour party was due to fly out. During his short spell with St Helens he'd won most things the game had to offer at the time including a Challenge Cup winners' medal at Wembley.

Paddy Kirwan

Of Irish decent? Actually born in Oldham in 1961.
Clubs: Oldham, Leigh
Playing era: 1979 - 1991
Position: Scrum half
Fame game: He scored the try that beat Wigan in the Challenge Cup one Sunday in 1987. The Colliers weren't beaten again in the competition for another nine years.
Retirement: Paddy had to give up his playing career because his studies took priority. He was taking a series of professional examinations which have certainly paid off in the long run.

What did he study? Civil Engineering at UMIST (that's University of Manchester Institute of Science and Technology) and he graduated with his degree in 1982.
Clever boy: With that he went to work for the Department of Transport and then he moved to work for companies in the private sector.
And what does he do today? He's the engineer in charge of Britain's motorways.
He's always late for work then? He puts in plenty of consumer research as his job, enjoys covering the whole of the country and driving on motorways.
He must be pretty stressed out with that then? He finds coaching a way to relieve it. Today he's coaching down at National Conference League club Saddleworth Rangers.
How did he end up there? You go up the M6. I suppose he'll have a plentiful supply of cones for the training sessions.

Phil Larder MBE

Age: 62.
Lookslike: Ageing fashion designer.
Era: 1967 – 1981.
Position: Centre.
Player at: Oldham, Whitehaven
Strengths: Pace and passing.
Folklore: He's also author of the RL coaching bible. I still read it every night.
Weaknesses: Not the biggest tackler.
Retired: 1981.
After playing? Coaching with Widnes, Keighley Cougars and Sheffield Eagles. The top job in GB coaching terms came in 1995 and he nearly won the RL World Cup but his downfall came when GB & Ireland went to New Zealand in 1996. The Lions lost all three Tests.

Switching codes: Phil went to the dark side in 1997 when he joined Clive Woodward's England management team as defensive coach. He actually was part of the set up who won the World Cup in 2003. Not bad eh, but it wasn't a job for life. Woodward quit for a life with the softies in football, and in 2006 Larder got the boot.

What was his League career highlight?: *"Being part of the Keighley Cougars set up when they won the old style Second Division. I always thought it was wrong they were either not promoted or given their opportunity when Super League was formed."*

What's he doing today? If you do accidentally catch union on Sky, you'll see him sitting alongside the Worcester Head Coach. He does have a good club rugby pedigree from his three years with Leicester Tigers.

Does he have any contact with league anymore? One of his two sons, David, plays back row forward with Halifax.

What about a league comeback? Will Ellery Hanley become Prime Minister?

Spare time: Along with wife Anne, they have invested in a Spanish property and like to spend time topping up their tans.

Brian Lockwood

Age: 60.

Clubs: Castleford, Canterbury-Bankstown, Balmain, Wakefield Trinity, Hull KR, Oldham and Widnes.

Era: Put it this way he still remembers the premier of that rugby league film with Richard Harris.

Never to be seen at...: Wheldon Road, Castleford – or The Jungle depending on which era you like your rugby. He fell out with the club in a row over money and has never set foot in the ground ever since.

Not the sort of thing you could sort out in the car park? *"I was promised a benefit and the club changed its mind; then I was promised a part of the deal that took me to Australia. That never happened so I've never been back to club."*

How influential was Brian? Up to the early 1970s, Great Britain could beat Australia in Test series. And then they signed some of the best British players of the time to teach them to play the game. These days, we can't beat them at any price.

Locky the businessman: One of a legion of Yorkshire-based players who have done well in the licensing trade. Today, he's got an interest in a boozer in Howden, East Yorkshire having run pubs around Wakefield ever since he retired as a player. He sold one of his pubs for £1 million.

So what's he doing now? Well, he can't stop mixing sport and business because he's taken over as steward at Pontefract Golf Club – he's also a playing member with a single-figure handicap.

Locky on League: *"I've had loads of enquiries about me going back into rugby. Clubs want me to take on advisory roles but I haven't heard anything that really interested me yet."*

Paul Loughlin

Age: 41.
Pronounced: Loff-lin.
Born: St Helens.
Clubs: St Helens, Bradford Northern, Huddersfield Giants, Swinton Lions.
Playing era: 1983 – 2001.
Final hooter: Yet another product of 1980s Rugby League who left hanging up his boots until the last minute.
How old? 35.
Career: His retirement was also hastened by the fact he had a production job offer from Pilkington's Glass in St Helens and that was just too tempting to miss.

He gave all that up to work in a glass factory. That's like Kylie Minogue jacking in singing and going to work as a dinner lady ? He's a realist. He wasn't going to able to play on for ever.
What does he do there? He helps make glass. Did you know the company invented self-cleaning glass.
How does that work? You'll have to ask Paul the next time you see him.
Top moments: Paul still rates signing for St Helens in 1983 as one of his best moments in the game because he didn't think he'd ever get the chance to join his boyhood heroes. He also recalls with great satisfaction scoring an interception try in a Test match against Australia and also being selected for the 1992 tour of Papua New Guinea, Australia and New Zealand. He didn't see the New Zealand leg because he broke his arm in the 'Battle of Parkes' when the New South Wales Country team coach yelped about the strong arm tactics of the British Lions, but it was the Brits had a number of players with serious injuries, including Paul with a broken arm.
Sport: Sunday morning golf. He has a handicap of 19.
Secret soccer star: He's been the goalkeeper for Garswood United Veterans team. He made the headlines of the 'Warrington Guardian' newspaper in 2007 when he was promoted to the club's first team to cover an injury crisis and in one game he saved a penalty as the team won 2-1.

Phil Lowe

Age: Peter Sterling add Luke Robinson minus Wally Lewis divided by The Queen times Brian Noble.

Real name: Philip Lowe

Clubs: Hull KR and Manly Warringah.

0-60 (yards): 3 minutes.

Playing era: 1966 – 1983

Retired: 1983.

How did Phil make his name? He wasn't a bad player but he made the inside pages of the newspapers too. Allegedly, accusations of a complicated love life surfaced in the Sunday paper the 'News of the World'

(allegedly) while he was away with the Great Britain team in Australia, allegedly.

A love rat? The reporters waited until he was safely out of the country before publishing the story. He's a big lad after all.

Other sporting talent: Before he signed for Hull KR he was a basketball player as well as a discus and hurdles champion at school.

A World Cup hero: Phil was a member of the last Great Britain team to win the rugby league World Cup in 1972. He was in the same team as Sky TV commentator Mike Stephenson.

Life after playing: Today Phil is a successful publican and hotelier in Hull.

And in Rugby League: He's put his money where his mouth for Rovers. He is on the Board of Directors at Hull KR as the Director of Rugby.

Ian Lucas

Age: 39.
Born: Wigan.
Club: Wigan.
Position: Utility forward.

A jack of trades and a master of none? Ian's playing career was cut short by a horrendous Paul Harragon tackle in the first Test at Sydney Football Stadium in 1992. Ian was left with a permanent neck injury.

Was he insured? Only up to the shoulders.

Ancient bits: When Ian was a player he was an antique dealer and had a shop in Wigan. But he gave it up to concentrate on playing and couldn't buy it back when his playing career was cut short.

Did he sell any Rugby League memorabilia? Like Henderson Gill gumshields? Maurice Bamford flat caps? No.

So what did he do? Ian went to work as a sales team manager for a mail order company in Manchester, but at the first opportunity he chucked it all in to go back into league as coach at Leigh.

I suppose with a bad neck he didn't look back: He'd gained experience working with Andy Gregory at Salford and used the time created by an eight-match ban for a high tackle on Ian Blease at Salford to study for his coaching qualification.

Is that all it takes, eight weeks? It was intensive.

Did he put the qualification to good use? Not at Leigh. He fell out with the club and he's never been back since. Not that he doesn't like the game, he just doesn't have the spare time any more.

Career: After splitting from Leigh, Ian went to work in the financial services sector until one day he bought one of his client's shop and office fitting businesses.

The game: Ian still sees and likes the game on television but the attraction of spending time with his family in their caravan in North Wales is greater.

Let me go tell Brian Noble that: Be my guest.

Joe Lydon

DOB: 26 November 1963
Born: Wigan.
Another Wiganer. What do they put in the water over there? He also played for Wigan. And Widnes, Eastern Suburbs (aka Sydney Roosters)
Playing era: 1981 – 1994.
Position: Centre three quarter, wing, fullback.
Where are you most likely to see Joe? On TV where he's now a dual code commentator.
Lives: Near Blackburn.
Historic: Joe was the subject of Rugby League's first £100,000 transfer when he moved from

Widnes to Wigan. His departure caused coach Eric Hughes to resign.
Management: After Wigan as a player, he moved into club management becoming Wigan's team manager. After two years Joe moved across the Pennines to live in fashionable north Leeds when he was appointed as the RFL's first-ever Technical Director.
What were his duties? Don't ask, it's too technical.
Didn't he go darkside? He was appointed as England's seven-a-side team coach in 2001 and almost three years later he became the full England team's backs coach.
Back on the job market: When Andy Robinson got the boot from international duty so did Joe.
Consultant: During 2007 Joe started work with Waterloo Rugby Club (they're based in north Liverpool) as a performance consultant.
Currently: Residing in the Harlequins league office, working closely alongside the Business Development Manager, and generally making life in the office that little bit more interesting.
Working life: Joe is a qualified Graphic Artist.
Dinner guest: If you could choose any top rugby people to be guests at a dinner table, make sure that you invite Joe Lydon because he is one of the great rugby conversationalist.
Wembley: Aged 11, Joe played in the first ever Challenge Cup curtain raiser.

John Mantle

Age: Where's my bus pass?

Born: Cardiff

Clubs: St Helens, Salford, Leigh, Barrow, Keighley, Oldham, Blackpool.

Sounds like a tour schedule for Joe Longthorne. What was his era? 1964 to 1982.

Position: Second row forward.

Status: One of the best ever forward signings from Welsh rugby union.

Games: 596

The big switch: St Helens did the best undercover job and brought him to the professional game.

Secret: Wigan had been chasing him too.

Wigan chase everyone. What about work? John was a teacher but didn't accept St Helens' contract until he'd been north for a job interview and got a job. He stayed teaching in and around St Helens until he retired.

Health: John's had one replacement knee joint and its fast becoming the time for it to be replaced. There was talk of him having to have the other knee joint traded in but he's kept that one at bay.

How's he done that? John and his daughter took a sports therapy course a couple of years ago and they both qualified. John then bought a small piece of equipment and started treating himself.

Blimey that's a bit drastic: *"I get about and play a bit of golf with former League players Bob Welding and Ken Williams so it's looking good for the moment."*

Head Taff: John was captain of the Welsh team in the infamous 'Battle of Brisbane' when the Welsh beat the English in the World Championship and effectively spiked the English team's title dreams.

Barrie McDermott

DOB: 22 July 1972.
Born: Oldham.
Appearance: A Russian Oligarch.
Clubs: Oldham, Wigan, Leeds, Bramley, Widnes.
Position: Prop.
Leading with his chin: In his autobiography 'Made for Rugby' Barrie revealed that he had lived life to the full and triumphed over adversity. He lost an eye in a shooting accident when he was 15 years old; achieved notoriety by being the first person to be CS gassed by the Police when he was arrested in 1996 and arrest-ed again for skipping bail when he returned from an Leeds away fixture. Add into that mix the losses of more than 40 games through suspension and a well documented rivalry with Bradford Bulls prop Stuart Fielden, then you have one of the toughest forwards to play during Super League's first dozen years.

Sounds like a plot for Die Hard 7: He would do all his own stunts too.

And today? Barrie is one of the game's most engaging personalities and a settled family man.

In business: Before becoming a full-time professional player Barrie was a joiner. At the time of writing he is a member of the Headingley development staff where he works with the new young stars for Leeds Rhinos.

And part-time? He's doing match commentary for Sky with big mate Terry O'Conner.

New dimension: If you're running a function and are looking for an accomplished after-dinner speaker then Barrie Mac is your man. He's much in demand around the northern sports club circuit.

Jim Mills

Age: 63.
Born: Aberdare, Wales.
Clubs: Halifax, Salford, Bradford Northern, North Sydney, Widnes (three times), Workington Town.
Playing era: 1964 – 1980.
Nickname: Big Jim.
School: The old school.
He secretly must have wanted to live in Leeds! Why's that then?
Because he had more than 20 trips to meet the Rugby League's Disciplinary Committee at RFL headquarters in Leeds. *"It was mistaken identity most of the time!"*

The same defence as OJ: When he was playing he tipped the scales at 17 and half stone and was six foot four inches tall. Not a man to be taken lightly.
International relations: Jim was banned from entering New Zealand for a while after an incident involving a New Zealand Test forward called John Greengrass.
What did Jim do for work while he was playing? He made a career working with a couple of breweries.
I like him: After they were closed he became a gas fitter. In Australia he worked as a lorry crewman for a waste paper company and then went back to work in a brewery when he got back to the UK to play for Widnes. Towards the end of his playing career he bought a night club in Widnes and it was called, appropriately enough; 'Big Jim's'.
I think I met my future ex-wife there: When he finished playing he joined the Widnes committee which eventually became the Board of Directors.
Health: Jim underwent heart bypass surgery in 2007 and part of his recovery plan was taking a train from his home in Frodsham, Cheshire to Llandudno in North Wales to walk round the Great Orme!

Roger Millward MBE

Age: 59.

Looks like: Accountant turned actor.

Stature: Small but powerful.

Clubs: Castleford, Hull KR, Cronulla-Sutherland (Australia)

Era: 1964 – 1980.

Fame at last: One of the first to get recognised by the Queen for services to RL in 1982.

What else happened in 1982? The sin bin was introduced.

Retired: Roger decided it was time to finish as a player when he suffered four broken jaws in ten months.

Ouch!: Roger's life hasn't been a bed of roses and thankfully he's fought and won a battle against cancer.

What did he do for a living? When he first left school like so many other lads brought up in Castleford he went down the pit. He trained as a colliery electrician.

A bright spark: He quit to be the full-time coach at Hull KR. At the end of his career, he had a brief spell as a Transport Manager and then he became the Premises Manager – a caretaker to our older readers – at Royd's School, Rothwell, West Yorkshire.

He threw away all that league experience? Not entirely. After he left Hull KR he had a brief spell at Halifax and that wasn't the happiest of times.

Why? *"My original plan after leaving Rovers was to take a year out of the game and go back fresh. When I went to Halifax it wasn't the right time or the right place."*

So what's his connection these days? In 2000 he was elected to British Rugby League's Hall of Fame and he still watches the odd match. Occasionally it is his home-town club Castleford but in 2007 he spent more time going back to Craven Park.

What were the highlights of his career? Obviously the Test series win in Australia in 1970 and winning the Challenge Cup Final against Hull FC when, after a tackle by Ronnie Wileman, he suffered a broken jaw. He showed his courage in that game playing on with the injury until the final whistle.

Mick Morgan

Age: 58.
Born: Featherstone.
Clubs: Wakefield Trinity, Featherstone Rovers, Carlisle, Oldham, Castleford.
Playing era: 1965 – 1989.
Retirement: Although Mick officially retired as a player with a worn out body in 1989. But his final, final game of rugby league was for Castleford's reserves in 1994.
Working life: When Mick was a player he worked at Ackton Hall Colliery in Featherstone where he was the pit top shunter.
What's a shunter? Coal was carried out of the pit on wagons and Mick was responsible for the movement out of all the coal.
So I have to thank him for my coal fire? He was also the pit top official for the National Union of Mineworkers.
He'll have been good mates with King Arthur then? They used to go to the ballet together. Arthur did okay out of the mining industry and has a lovely big holiday home in Ireland.
Changes: When the collieries closed Mick became the fund raiser at Oldham.
Back to Yorkshire: In 1986 he was recruited by Castleford to join them as a player and their fund raiser. He helped establish the commercial department at Wheldon Road.
Raconteur: Mick became one of Rugby League's best known voices on the after dinner speaking circuit as an auctioneer selling off sporting memorabilia for good causes, usually players' testimonial funds.
Road Show: Morgan's auction spiel was laced with stories, which made him in much demand. He was a central character in the Sunday Mirror Rugby League Road Show that made more than £100,000 for players' testimonial funds in 100 outings.
Today: Mick is Mine Host at the Oddfellows Arms at Sherburn in Elmet near Castleford and many of his regular customers are Rugby League men.

Keith Mumby

Age: 50.
Born: Spennymore, Co. Durham
Clubs: Bradford Northern, Sheffield Eagles, York, Keighley, Wakefield Trinity.
Position: Full-back.
Playing era: 1973 – 1993.
Child prodigy: Went into the Bradford team as a teenager and stayed there.
Biggest shock: When his beloved Northern told him he could leave the club.
Fitting the joint: All the way through his playing career Keith was a joiner and he's still cutting a mean piece of timber as a self employed woodworker today.

Does he do commissions like Lord Linley? I dare say he could knock you up an oak cabinet for your gun room but he mainly does odds and sods around the house.
Does he take his cabinet making skills to Odsal? He's one of those players who doesn't like being a spectator.
Staying in touch: Keith occasionally gets suited and booted and goes to Bradford's Ex-Players 'do's. In fact he was one of the former Northern stars who turned out for the club's centenary dinner in 2007.
Happy days: Keith was at his happiest in the Northern dressing room but he admits that he wasn't the greatest of trainers.
Travel woe: One of the reasons that he didn't like the training regime was that he had to finish work and get home. Then he'd have to jump the number 80 bus, do the business with the players and then dash off for his bus home.
Greatest moments: Not surprisingly, Keith picks out his best moment as signing for Bradford Northern when coach Ian Brooke and late chairman Harry Womersley got him to sign on the dotted line for the Odsal club. He is also proud to have played for his country eleven times, including being a Great Britain tourist in 1989.

Craig Murdock

DOB: 24 October 1973
Born: Whitehaven
Clubs: Wigan, Hull FC, Salford, Keighley Cougars, Hull KR.
Playing era: 1993 – 2003.
Position: Scrum half.
Why didn't he ever play for a Cumbrian club? None were interested in signing him. He'd been on the BARLA tour to Australia and returned to join Wigan. Why wouldn't you play for them?
What happened to make him retire? He snapped his Achilles tendon.
Nasty: *"I was never the same* 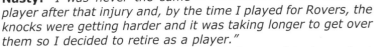 *player after that injury and, by the time I played for Rovers, the knocks were getting harder and it was taking longer to get over them so I decided to retire as a player."*
Coaching: He was due to be appointed as assistant coach at Hull KR but when Steve Linnane was replaced by Harvey Howard the club did not offer a job to Craig.
So that was it? Out of the blue he got an offer from BBC Radio Humberside to go for an audition as a summariser for the match commentary team.
Did he get the job except for the fact he kept referring to the coach as 'that Aussie bastard?' No, they get on.
Nice: *"I'd given a few interviews to the station when I played at Hull FC and Hull KR so they knew what I sounded like. I went for the audition and the rest, as they say, is history. I've been doing it for almost five years and really enjoy the job."*
But wouldn't that mean he only works at the weekend? When Craig was at home in Cumbria he was an electrician at the atomic power station at Sellafield. After five years as a full-time player, he went to work as a hospital engineer and that's what he's doing today.
His day job you mean? He's in charge of Hull Royal Infirmary's X-Ray machines – among other things – and that means he often comes face-to-face with some of the current players as they pass through the department after an injury.

Alex Murphy OBE

DOB: 22/4/1939.
Born: St Helens.
Clubs: St Helens. Leigh, Warrington.
Position: Scum half, stand off, centre.
Retired: 1975.
Painful decision: After his second broken jaw of his career.
If there was a Hollywood film of him...: Alex would be played by Roy Scheider.
Careers advice: At school Murphy told everyone he was going to be involved in rugby league and guess what...he still is.

Management style: He shouts a lot from the dugout. He was a bit of a cocky lad and always full of himself but it worked.
Work: When Alex left school he trained to be a joiner and worked at various collieries.
Then: After going to work for Pilkington's, Alex decided to set up his own joinery business and was making good progress until he signed for Cronulla. He'd sold his business but the deal fell through.
On the move: In 1970 he went to be coach at Leigh and led them to a Challenge Cup win over Leeds at Wembley in 1971. Then he became player-coach at Warrington and created a dynasty of glory through the 1970s. That was followed by coaching jobs at Salford, Wigan and Huddersfield.
And today? He's a professional after-dinner speaker, a business he's maintained for the last 20 years. He even has his own website where you can book him for your very own function.
Meeting Her Majesty: *"The Queen said she'd never seen me at Wembley and I replied 'No but your mum did'. Then she asked if she would ever see me there again. I said it was doubtful, unless I was sat next to her in the Royal Box."*
Any other honours? He was voted player of the Millennium by Rugby Leaguer.
Lives: Near St Helens.

Martin Murphy

Age: 59
Born: Very young.
Playing era: 1966 – 1982
Club: Oldham, Newtown Jets.
Games: 461.
Position: Full back.
Club man: Murphy went to Oldham in 1966 and stayed there until his face didn't fit in 1982.
Why, did it grow into an odd shape? Merely a figure of speech. He could have left when his home-town club Leigh showed some interest in him in 1970, but he chose to stay.
Loyalty: *"At the time Leigh were interested in me it was suggested to me that I might like to be awkward with Oldham and stay away from the club to make a transfer more likely. But I could never have done that because the Oldham fans had been so good to me and they paid to see us play each week. It wouldn't have been fair."*
Work: When Martin first left school he served his time as a tool maker and then after having several other jobs he ended up buying two window cleaning rounds in Oldham. And he's still climbing those ladders today.
Any scary moments? He's had a couple of hairy moments but likely he's still at it, shammy in hand.
Highlights: The view into number 53 can be good at times. In rugby, it was being made club captain at Oldham as well as playing a couple of times for Lancashire and once for England in 1975.
Currently: Martin's not able to get to many games these days because he is looking after his wife Anne who suffered a brain haemorrhage eight years ago and is now wheelchair-bound. But when he can he drops in to watch his former club as they continue their battle to return to the game's elite level.

Tony Myler

Age: 46.
Born: Widnes
Club: Widnes - another one-club man.
Retired: 1993.
Position: Stand off half.
Rating: Tipped to be the superstar of the era but had a dodgy back.
Coaching: In 1994, Widnes invited him to become the club's first-team coach.
What went wrong after that? Widnes brought Doug Laughton back into the team management team and that spelt trouble at at' mill.

Get it off your chest, Tony: *"I thought we were doing OK. I had my brother assisting me and his knowledge of the game was respected throughout the sport. We'd won the games we expected to win and I didn't think we needed any help."*
And afterwards? Well, Tony still thinks that Widnes made a mistake and points to the large number of coaches the club's appointed since then.
How many? 536.
Today: Tony's an occasional golf player at Widnes Golf Club. But his business commitments have limited his appearances on the course.
As a what? He works in the family engineering business.
Career highlights: For Tony playing in a winning World Club Challenge team for Widnes against Canberra Raiders at Old Trafford, Manchester in 1991 was the ultimate club experience, while his first selection for Great Britain also ranks near the top for him.
Touring: Tony was selected for the 1984 Great Britain tour of Australia and New Zealand but injured his right knee in a Challenge Cup semi-final. He managed to pass the fitness test to make the trip but says it was a mistake to go.
Lives: Widnes.
Has he got any of his old shirts? They were never in any fit state to be kept.

Steve Nash

Age: 58.
Born: Featherstone.
Clubs: Featherstone Rovers, Salford, Rochdale Hornets, Mansfield Marksmen.
Isn't there another Steve Nash who plays? He currently plays for Salford after pledging his life to Widnes.
Old Steve's playing era: 1967 – 1986.
Finished: Steve finally severed his connections with the game after a spell coaching Rochdale amateur club Mayfield, but his playing career had come to an end after a brief period with the

one-time Nottinghamshire club, Mansfield Marksmen.
Staying in the game: Steve was gainfully employed during his playing days as a bricklayer but no more.
Health problems: Steve had his injury problems while playing, including a detached retina, and today Steve is retired and living in Rochdale. His working life had been brought to a premature end by illness and he's had quadruple heart bypass surgery.
That must have been a shock? He had a heart attack pushing a wheel-barrow full of bricks up a plank of wood.
I've seen that. It's a disaster waiting to happen: The thing was he never realised he was having one at the time.
What were the highlights of his playing career? Playing in the 1972 World Cup with Great Britain and for Featherstone at Wembley are his top moments. *"It was an amazing experience playing for Great Britain when I was just 24 years old. We went to France and came back as winners having drawn with Australia in the World Cup Final. It was a real privilege to be in that side."* Then a year later he was named as the winner of the Lance Todd Trophy as Man of the Match when Featherstone Rovers beat Bradford Northern at Wembley.

Paul Newlove

Age: 36.

Blimey, still a young guy: He was just 32 when he retired due to a foot injury.

His Hollywood biog would be played by: Charlie Sheen.

Born: Pontefract (12,659 miles from Hollywood).

Clubs: Featherstone Rovers, Bradford Bulls, St Helens, Castleford Tigers.

Playing era: 1989 – 2004

Position: Centre.

Games: 476.

Work: For many years Paul was a full-time player but today he is a Student Liaison Officer with a

school in Wakefield. Paul didn't have any real plans for the future when he left Rugby League but he's been enjoying this challenging role in education for the last three years.

Does he still shove loads of Brylcream on his hair? Whether it was a tactic or a fashion statement, he did seem to wear a lot of Brylcream on the pitch, but it's gone the way of smoking - not really the done thing in the office.

How was he rated ? One of the most gifted players of his generation. That was illustrated by the fact that St Helens were prepared to give Bradford a deal worth a then world record £500,000 for him.

Caps: Paul played 20 times for Great Britain.

Why you won't see him at matches: *"I don't get that many free tickets these days."*

Mike Nicholas

Age: 60
Born: Port Talbot, South Wales.
That's home to the largest refinery works in the UK: Aye, Mike was a pretty refined player too.
Clubs: Warrington, Cardiff Blue Dragons.
Era: 1972 – 1981.
Not another rugby player who came from the Valleys and pledged himself to league but only did so because he couldn't get a game playing union? Mike was recruited for Warrington by Alex Murphy so he got a good start in life up north.

So he's done the game proud? He's no mug. He bought a one-acre plot of land in one of Warrington's leafy suburbs, and established a garage business.

Didn't he do taxis too? He may have picked you up as 'Wire Wheels'.

What's he up to do these days? He's got loads of interests.

Such as? A celebrity website business, corporate entertaining interests and runs an event management company. He's also into management services. If you need a boss look no further than Nicko.

I am exhausted: He even had a 12-year stint as manager of the Welsh national team and took them to the 1995 World Cup semi-final and the 2000 World Cup semi-final against Australia.

But no more? He's too busy. He's the President of Wales Rugby League and trying to develop the sport in the Principality. Among the projects he's been working on is a £2 million plus League Academy in the Valleys plus an eight team amateur league operating along the south Welsh coast.

George Nicholls

Age: 63.
Born: Widnes.
Clubs: Widnes, St Helens, Cardiff Blue Dragons, Salford.
Playing era: 1962 – 1983.
Retirement: George put his original retirement plans on hold after answering an appeal from Salford's David Watkins.
What appeal? To sell poppies?: Watkins helped get Cardiff Blue Dragons off the ground in 1981 and recruited George when he found out he was leaving St Helens.
So George headed to the Valleys? He had one year at Cardiff and then another year at Salford.

What was his job when he was a player? George made a nice living as a scaffolder in the building trade. He worked on power stations at Fiddlers Ferry and Ince 'B' but once that work finished he had to do something else.
What did he do? He gained his HGV license and went to be a lorry driver.
So is he still eating the Yorkie bars? No. Three years ago his playing days caught up with him and he had to retire from work altogether.
He failed the MOT? A specialist advised George that he couldn't do any strenuous driving because he couldn't turn his neck properly. He has two vertebrae that have fused together.
Did he have any other major career injuries? Only a broken arm.
Does he have any connections with League today? Yes he does. He's the organiser of the Widnes Ex-Players Association and serves on the British Lions Association Committee.

Martin Offiah MBE

Age: 40.
Born: Hackney, London.
Clubs: Widnes, Wigan, London Broncos, Salford (plus Eastern Suburbs and St George in Australia).
Playing era: 1987 – 2000.
Where likely to be seen? London nightclubs, the theatre or locker rooms of west London gyms.
Nickname: Chariots.
Distinguishing feature: Big Nike tattoo on his left arm. Now that's what I call brand loyalty.
Best moves: Collects ball from own try line and races through

the opposition to score a try using his electric pace.
Retirement: Aged 33. Became a professional personality.
New career: Whenever you switched the telly on he seemed to be on our screens, one way or another.
Twinkle toes: But Martin's biggest break (after joining Widnes from Rosslyn Park rugby union club in 1987) was in 2003 when he danced to fourth place in the original series of the hit television programme 'Strictly Come Dancing'. It's a fair bet plenty of full backs he'd rounded in his rugby career could have vouched for his fancy footwork even before he hit the dance floor!
What other TV shows has he been on? 'Emmerdale', 'Hollyoaks', 'The Weakest Link', 'Stars in their Eyes', 'Jade's Salon', 'Comic Relief does Fame Academy', An Audience with Joe Pasquale', 'A Question of Sport', 'Top of the Pops Saturday', 'Hell's Kitchen' and 'Come African Dancing' – need we go on?
Martin did: He's been listed by one major web site as one of the 100 Black Britons of all time.
Who's top? Shirley Bassey.
Back to school: In May 2003 Martin studied drama and he has already appeared on stage to some acclaim in London.
Music: Martin's also launched into a career as a disc jockey. He's got a passion for house music and has already made a big impression as a DJ in London and other major cities in Britain.
Mastermind subject: World War II.

Steve O'Neill

Age: 49
Born: Widnes.
Clubs: Wigan, Widnes, Swinton, Salford
Playing era: 1975 – 1991
Blood dynasty: One of two brothers to make it in the professional game, Steve and Mike.
Work: While Steve was still playing, he worked as a roofer but then went into the pub game. And that's where he is today as landlord of the Appleton Arms in down town Widnes.

Coaching: Steve was on the coaching staff at Salford for many years and also moved into the international arena when he took charge of the Ireland team that did so well in the 2000 World Cup.
Why's he not still in the game? *"To keep that kind of international team job you had to have a club affiliation and I lost the Irish post when I left Salford."*
What about seeing his former team-mates? He's in regular contact with their Michael who now lives in Liverpool but doesn't see many of his generation of Widnes players much. *"We get together at Widnes games now and again but now as often as we should."*
Highlights: Steve's favourite Rugby League memories are focussed on Widnes's Challenge Cup exploits. He remembers his first semi-final in 1982 when Mick Adams had a kick rebound off the cross bar to provide the winning try. Steve got his winner's medal when Widnes beat his former club Wigan in 1984 thanks to two long-distance Joe Lydon tries.
Friendship: Steve and Aussie centre Steve Rogers both broke their legs in the same game at Wigan and ended up in adjoining hospital beds. Their friendship forged in that adversity lasted through until Rogers' untimely death in 2006.

Geoff Pimblett

Age: 63.
That's what we like, a good old rugby player's name. He got it from his father.
Born: St Helens.
Club: St Helens.
A one-man club? Why bother playing anywhere else?
Playing era: 1971 – 1979
Calling it quits: Being dropped from the side was all he needed.
Why did he sign for Saints? Why not. Better than Hunslet.
Working life: When he was a rugby union player, he trained to be a teacher. He went to teach history at Grange Park School in St Helens.
And today? Geoff took retirement from the teaching profession several years ago and now he's part of the community programme at Knowsley Road.
What does he do for the club? Two days a week he goes down to the stadium and gives school children a tour round the ground. He then links that to giving talks about the club, the game and the town. It gives the kids a great perspective on how the club and the sport have become important to St Helens and its citizens.
Wembley Magic: Two great highlights stand out in Geoff's Rugby League career. The first was playing in the 1976 Challenge Cup Final at Wembley. That was the day when temperatures out on the pitch soared to more than 100 degrees and Saints got up to beat Widnes 20-5 with Geoff named the winner of the Lance Todd Trophy as Man of the Match.
England expects: His second highlight was playing for his country, England, in an international, appropriately for Geoff at St Helens, in 1978. He said: *"I was only selected once but it was a great honour and we had a big win over Wales."*

Harry Pinner

Age: 50.
Is he from Pinner? No, St Helens.
Clubs: St Helens, Widnes, Leigh, Bradford Northern, Carlisle.
Playing era: 1974 – 1987.
That's a good innings: Yep, 13 years.
Talent: Although not one of the biggest players in the game, Harry was known as clever footballer. His left foot had an IQ of 160.
Up north: The Pinner playing career came to an end in Cumbria after he signed for the

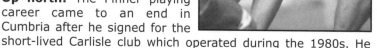

short-lived Carlisle club which operated during the 1980s. He played just 12 games for the club.
Why so few games? Harry was offered a job on the Wigan coaching staff working as an assistant with coach John Monie. Mind you Harry now believes that taking the job was a mistake.
Contract: Stage payments of £150 and £250 then £600 pounds when he had played 12 first-team games. As an incentive he was offered another £75 if he played for his county and a further £250 if he played for Great Britain. A total of £1,325!
What was his job in the real world? He was a driver for the local council but when he turned 25 he decided to become a publican. He eventually took over the Parr Arms in Warrington and made it into a very desirable hostelry. However, following a period of ill health he sold his business and went into a well-earned retirement.
Did he move far away? No. Towards the end of his playing career he was granted a testimonial by St Helens and he invested the money earned from that fund in buying a cottage near Warrington. And that's where he went to live.
How will he spend his time? He's got plenty to think about but he will go back to his hobby....breeding bulldogs!
Bloody horrible things. I'd ban them! Cars do more damage than dogs and you couldn't do without one of them.
That's okay then: He's also hoping to spend more time on the customer side of the Parr Arms bar.

Steve Pitchford

Age: 55
Born: Hunslet, Leeds.
AKA: The Hulk of Hunslet.
Clubs: Leeds, Bramley.
Playing era: 1965 -1984.
Position: Prop forward
Game Style: The ultimate pocket battleship. Low centre of gravity and loads of power.
Twin retirements: The first time he quit was after Leeds signed a load of players from Australia. And the second time was when the Bramley club signed loads of players from Bramley.
Sport: Steve's transferred his sporting affections over to golf.
Another Tiger? *"I'm a bit on the rotund side so my swing isn't all that great but I'm pretty nifty around the putting greens."*
I'm thinking Mark Calcaveccia, Russell Clayden, John Daly: You wouldn't be far wrong.
Cheers! Having started his working life in engineering, during the time he was a player with Leeds, he became a pub landlord.
Where? Scarborough.
And today? He's the steward of Knaresborough Working Men's Club near Harrogate.
Career highlight: That 1977 Challenge Cup Final win over St Helens when he was the winner of the Lance Todd Trophy as man of the match. It was such a great performance that he was taken into the Great Britain tour team on the strength of that display when Warrington's Mike Nicholas had to pull out of the trip.
Happy memories: That same year Steve was also named as the Leeds club's 'Player of the Year'.
Strange fact: Although Steve became a league legend he played rugby union at school. Is that strange enough?

Andy Platt

Age: 43.
Born: St Helens.
Clubs: St Helens, Wigan, Auckland Warriors, Salford, Workington Town.
Position: Loose forward.
Playing era: 1983 - 2001.

Platt attack: Pre-full-time playing he'd worked as a steel erector in his uncle's firm but in retirement he's followed the time-honoured route by taking a pub, the Eagle and Child in Billinge (between St Helens and Wigan). When he went to work at Workington he returned to full-time Rugby League duties, but the pub experience came in handy later.

Didn't he play Down Under? Andy played with Brisbane briefly in 1985 and being in Australia he decided that's where his future lay. The decision made, he jetted to Sydney to start his new life.

New home: The hunt for a new home started when they landed in Oz and, after a spell living with friends in Sydney, the Platt family headed north up Australia's east coast to Brisbane.

Does he bump into Glen Lazarus? Not unless he stays with them because Andy and his wife bought a motel. Moves to Brisbane and Cairns followed but now they live in Townsville where he is working for a company that buys and sells motels, hotels and caravan sites.

Investment: While they have been moving around Queensland, the Platts took ownership of a motel in Mackay and, although it had been run for them by managers, they were due to take over the business themselves once they had returned from a visit to Britain in autumn 2007.

Do they do traditional English breakfasts? It's not a B&B. Motels are where sad people eat their breakfast in their cars.

How come Platty didn't finish as a player until 2001? He was an assistant coach with Brisbane Wests in the Queensland Cup competition and filled in when somebody was injured in the 'A' grade competition.

Scott Quinnell

Age: 35.
Born: Morriston, Swansea, Wales.
Club: Wigan Warriors.
Playing era: 1994 – 1997.
Shirt Size: XXXXXXL.
Joining league's 'Taffia': Scott came into the 13-man code after a number of high profile Welsh rugby union players had taken the decision to come north. Then came the professional union version game and its cash recovered him. League had just got him really fit and he left.
Are you saying he was a tub of lard when he came to rugby league? Fitness wasn't his forte.
Work: Today Scott has his own public relations company in South Wales which specialises in working on social issues. And he's also making a few bob working as a pundit with Sky Television.
Not bad for a man who can't read. I understand he has dyslexia? He's done very well and never let adversity get him down. He's actually promoting a technique to get kids overcoming their problems with dyslexia.
Why is it such a difficult word to spell? It's called the Dore technique. Some autographs hunters would throw their bits of paper back at him because he had spelt their name wrong.
How does the Dore work? The usual stuff. Standing on bean bags, throwing balls in the air.
Family life: Married to Nicola with three kids.
Favourite book: Richard Branson's autobiography.
Lives: Llanelli.
Back in union: After initially going back into union with Richmond – they paid Wigan £250,000 for him and later went under financially – Scott eventually returned to Llanelli and played for Wales and the British Lions.
Caps: 52.
Don't mention: The 2007 Rugby World Cup.

Dave Redfearn

Age: 55
Born: Birstall.
Club: Bradford Northern.
Playing era: 1968 – 1990.
Retired: 1990.
Why did you retire as a player? *"Well, I was 38 years old and, quite simply, I was knackered."*
And what happened after he finished playing? I became a self-employed electrician.
Still in contact with the great game? Only from the side lines because he's a floor manager with Sky Sports at Super League games.
How did he land that soft touch? Well, it was all down to former Huddersfield winger Peter Judge. When Dave retired Peter, who worked in Public Relations part time, approached him to see if he wanted do some PR work in other sports.
Then what happened? *"I went to work with Judgey for the Karen Earl organisation where we used to work for major sponsors like Silk Cut and Benson and Hedges at big sports events helping service the media and making sure the broadcasters got what they needed."*
Is that how he broke into television? Yes, he was taken on to be a floor manager and worked on the broadcasts when the Australian's toured this country and had their broadcasters sending pictures back Down Under.
What other sports has he worked on? *"Well, I've worked on broadcasts in Rugby Union, Soccer, Darts, Speedway and Ice Hockey."*
And his plum job: Well, Redders was nobody's mug on the field and he wasn't afraid of a bit of biff, so Sky knew what they were doing when they made him senior floor manager for their Boxing broadcasts for five years. Well, he was a bit tougher than some of the fighters and they wouldn't argue with him if they had any sense.

Malcolm Reilly OBE

Age: 59.
Born: Castleford
Playing era: 1967 -1986
Clubs: Castleford, Manly Warringah.
Position: Loose forward, prop forward
Honoured: Given the Order of the British Empire by Her Majesty the Queen in 1990 for his services to the sport.
Nickname: One Australian newspaper tagged him as the 'The Monster' which did not go down well with Reilly.
Work: Like so many other men from Castleford, Malcolm went to work down't pit. He was a welder and fitter and worked at the Ledston Luck Colliery. But once he joined Australian club Manly in 1971 he became a full-time player.
First love: Soccer. There I've said it.
Signing fee: He joined Castleford for £200 on 15 May 1967.
To Australia: After helping Castleford win the Challenge Cups in successive years in 1969, Reilly decided to emigrate to Australia and signed for Manly. He cost them 30,000 Aussie dollars but helped them to the 1972 and 1973 Premierships.
Coaching: Malcolm went on to coach at Leeds and Halifax as well as the Great Britain team. He returned to Australia where he took Newcastle Knights to the 1997 Australian premiership. Back to Britain to take over as coach at Huddersfield Giants. He was also Director of Rugby and Coach at Hull KR, his last full-time job in British Rugby League which he left in December 2004.
Where would you see Malcolm today? Probably walking the shores of Lake Macquarie near Newcastle in Australia. He left his home in Ledston near Castleford in 2006 and retired to his home in New South Wales.
Hobbies: Cooking. If you ever get invited round for dinner, he likes to make Chinese food.

Dean Sampson

DOB: 27 June 1967.
Born: Wakefield.
Clubs: Castleford Tigers, Hunslet, Gold Coast & Parramatta Eels.
Retired: 2002.
Lurking: He's not the sort of guy you would like to meet in a dark alley.
Nickname: Diesel.
Diesel? Guess what he put in a petrol car?
How come the name stuck. I've done that before and nobody calls me Diesel. His Dad was an assistant coach at Castleford at the time and he

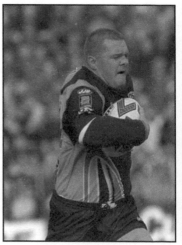

told the other players about Dean's mistake. *"From the moment I got to training, the lads were calling me 'Diesel', and it stuck for the rest of my career."*

Working: Before he became a full-time player with Cas, Dean just filled in time doing various jobs from working on a building site to being a fitness consultant at a leisure centre.

What happened after he finished playing? At first he worked for the RFL as a Player Performance Analyst, now he's a property developer and living in the Wakefield area.

He didn't think about opening a petrol station? No.

Coaching: Dean's no longer part of the scene but for a short spell he was a member of the coaching set up at Castleford and his last job in the game was as assistant coach at Hull KR.

Oh, the embarrassment: Dean laid out poor Willie Poching because he thought Willie had flattened his team-mate Brad Davis. What he didn't know was that Brad had been laying it on a bit thick for the benefit of the referee and just after Dean had delivered the knockout blow he realised that that Brad was standing just beside him.

No: *"I looked at Brad, realised what had happened and said to him, "you've just got me sent off!"*

What about poor Willie? *"I went to see Willie in the dressing room straight away and apologised to him. And being the bloke he is, he accepted my apology. I was still banned though."*

Garry Schofield OBE

Age: 42.
Look-alike: Shrek.
Born: Hunslet (the posh bit), Leeds.
Clubs: Hull FC, Leeds, Huddersfield Giants, Doncaster, Bramley.
This time next year: A future candidate for *Strictly Come Dancing*.
Playing era: 1983 – 1999.
Position: Stand off or centre.
Slim pickings: Amazingly Garry never won anything with a club.
Status: Surely Garry will be a candidate for the Sports Hall of Fame committee when they next

consider suitable candidates. He will have been retired from playing ten years in 18 months time and that's about the time the committee are due to sit again.
Popularity stakes: Garry was crossed off loads of Christmas card lists in Hull when he moved from FC to his home-city club Leeds for a then world record transfer fee of £155,000 in the 1987–88 season. While he wore the blue and amber he was branded as a 'traitor' by large sections of the Hull FC fans.
Dark side: Garry spent a successful spell of about a year playing centre for Welsh union outfit Aberavon.
Coaching: Schoey was player/coach with Huddersfield Giants from November 1997 until March 1998. After the Giants sacked him he spent two years coaching Redcar Rugby Union Club.
Punditry: He's a regular pundit for Sky Television, BBC television and BBC local radio stations while he also has his own column in the Daily Star and Sunday Star.
Money: After a spell running a boozer in Leeds, Garry's now back working as a bricklayer.
Honour: Garry was awarded the OBE by her Majesty the Queen in June 1994 for his services to Rugby League.
Would we recognise him today? He's filled out a bit but still has the moustache.

Glyn Shaw

Age: 56
Born: Neath, Wales
Clubs: Widnes, Wigan, Warrington, Rochdale Hornets, Runcorn Highfield.
Another Taff who played for Wigan: It's a multi-cultural game. You watch, the Polish will soon be playing for Wigan.
Like Radlinksi? The invasion has already started.
Playing era: 1977 – 1991.
Image: He looked like his craggy features were held together by a headband.
Retirement: Glyn's League playing career came to an end

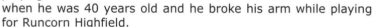

when he was 40 years old and he broke his arm while playing for Runcorn Highfield.
Spectacular: Glyn had a reputation for being a bit of an extrovert when he was relaxing and there are tales that he liked eating different foods, like budgies, but that's just a rumour, we're told.
That's definitely a headline for RL Express. What does he do for money? Glyn's been a self-employed welder and engineer for most of his life but recently he's become a maintenance engineer for some massive overhead cranes at a container depot in Widnes.
Going North: Glyn came north to play league because of financial inducements and curiosity. His career in union was all but over.
On the switch: *"As soon as I ran with the ball I knew it was the game for me. My way of playing was far more suited to the 13-man game."*
Coaching: Glyn has not been lost to the game because he has been helping with the fitness for Widnes amateur RL Club, West Bank Swans, and seeing that they have managed several successive promotions, he must be working well.

Kelvin Skerrett

Age: 41.
Born: Sunny Hunslet, Leeds. You can still buy a 2-bed house there for £13,000.
Clubs: Hunslet, Bradford Northern, Wigan Warriors, Halifax.
Era: 1981 – 1999.
Position: Prop or second row forward
Style: Like Darth Vadar on steroids.
Retirement: Kelvin was 35 years old - he just walked away from the game.
Without injury? *"I didn't advertise the fact that I'd*

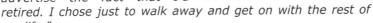

retired. I chose just to walk away and get on with the rest of my life."
You tell 'em Kelvin: Kelvin was a sheet metal worker but the company he worked for got so fed up with him taking time off because of rugby injuries that they gave him a choice - rugby or work.
I know which I would choose: *"It worked out well for me and I never regretted having to take that decision."*
Working life 2: In the end he moved into the licensed trade taking a pub called 'The Kingdom' in Methley near Castleford and he still lives in the village.
Building a new career: Kelvin then moved into the property development business and that is now an international affair for him.
So he's loaded? He's *le loaded*. Today he is building houses for sale in the South of France although he doesn't have any plans to move there himself.
How much would a little love nest cost? If you had a spare half a million euros you might get something with a view. Still he can fly down to Nice whenever he fancies a bit of sun and watch over his developments.

Trevor Skerrett

Age: 54
Born: Hunslet, Leeds.
Clubs: Wakefield Trinity, Hull
FC, Leeds, Keighley
Playing era: 1974 – 1989
Positions: Second row forward
and prop forward.
Game style: Strong as an ox.
Retirement: Doctors advice.
*"Mr Skerrett with the state of
your knees not only shouldn't
you play next year, you
shouldn't have played last year
either!"*
Retirement: 1988-89 season.
Afterwards he signed on for the
famous Hunslet area club Bison

Sports and played seven more seasons with them.
Working life: He started his working life as a bricklayer and
then moved into the pub game. He was mine host at the Bay
Horse at Meanwood in Leeds until a couple of years ago but has
now returned to his original trade as a bricklayer.
**He could build houses in the South of France for his
nephew, Kelvin:** The offer hasn't come in yet but I will pass on
the sentiment.
Replacements: In 2006 he had both knees replaced.
We never said RL was a girls game: Twice injuries robbed
Trevor of glory. He missed a Wembley appearance after
snapping his Achilles tendon six days before the Final and he
was named as captain of the Great Britain team to tour Australia
in 1984 but had to pull out with injury. He was replaced as
skipper by Bradford Northern hooker Brian Noble.
Top Taff: When the 1978 Australian touring team came to the
UK, Trevor wanted to play against them. He was not included in
the Yorkshire squad or their shadow squad to face the
Kangaroos, so he declared himself available for Wales because
his mum was Welsh. He got the chance to play against Australia
for Wales and emerged as joint Man of the Match with Aussie
halfback Tommy Ravdonikis.

Alan Smith

Age: 63
Club: Leeds
Born: Overton, Wakefield.
Playing era: 1962 – 1983
Position: Wing man.

How did it all end? On a stretcher. Alan damaged his knee during a Wednesday night match at Widnes the end of the 1982-83 season.

Coaching: Immediately after he retired as a player Alan helped coach David Ward with the coaching at Leeds but decided that player management was not for him.

Business life: In the aftermath of his career Alan was considering a life in physiotherapy but then came an offer he just couldn't refuse.

Quality control manager at Tetley's brewery? No, no. A mate of his knew he was at a loose end and that he had accountancy skills. So he asked Alan to join him in a business venture in the plumbing and heating trade. And that lasted until 2007 as he started to wind down his working life when he and his business partner sold the business.

Likes: Walking and biking.

Highlights: For Alan the two things that stand out in his playing career are; playing in the Challenge Cup Final at Wembley in 1968 – the infamous 'water splash' Final between Leeds and Wakefield when Don Fox missed a last-minute goal kick in front of the posts and lost the opportunity to win the game for Trinity – and, being selected for the 1970 tour of Australia and New Zealand.

Kurt Sorensen

Age: 50.

Hang on a minute! I thought this book was about the whereabouts of GB players? It was, but I got a call from Down Under, and we've been asked to do a book of ex-players from the southern hemisphere too. This is a little taster.

Who's writing it? I don't know yet but if you know of anyone who knows Peter Sterling, Wally Lewis or Mal Meninga then tell them to get in touch.

So what about Kurt? He played for Wigan and Widnes.

Alternative career: WWE wrestler.

Born: Auckland, New Zealand.

Retired: 1995 - although some of his tackles are still felt today.

Reputation: He had arms like lamp-posts.

Working in England: Kurt's a brickie by trade and he worked for several companies around Widnes then he decided to go into the nightclub business.

Did Kurt work the door? No, although you never got any trouble at his clubs.

Today, where could I go and have a drink with Kurt? He's working in the building industry near his home on Queensland's Gold Coast.

There's an irony. He could run through them as a player now he builds them. Surely his playing days are long passed? Kurt puts his boots on now and again as he's part of a large New Zealand Rugby League ex-patriot population in and around the Gold Coast and they play veteran internationals against Australian vet sides as part of the fund raising effort for Australia's homeless and needy.

Kids: Tyler and Tayler.

Spoken in a Kiwi accent they sound the same. Is it confusing at meal times? No, they're grown up now making their way in the world.

Career highlight: Playing for New Zealand.

Gary Stephens

Age: 53.
Born: Castleford.
Clubs: Castleford, Manly Warringah, Wigan, Halifax, York
Playing era: 1969 – 1987.
Wind down: Gary's body started to crumble when he was player-coach at York in the late 1980s.
Retired: Aged 35.
Coaching: Gary was his own boss at York and then he went into a spell when he was an assistant coach at some of the biggest clubs in the game. Doug Laughton at Leeds, Malcolm Reilly at Halifax and John Joyner

at Castleford. But after his time working on the staff at his home-town club he left the game behind.
Cleaning up: While he was a player Gary had several businesses including a carpet cleaners. He was an insurance salesman and the owner of an industrial cleaning outfit.
Work: Today Gary, who still lives in Castleford, has returned to his original trade as welder and is now a contractor in the business.
Highlights: Gary gained five Great Britain caps in 1979. They were all won away from home and those are among his prized possessions. He is also one of the few English players to have won the Australian Grand Final. During his spell with Manly in 1979, when he was playing alongside Steve Norton and Phil Lowe for the Sea Eagles, they went all the way and beat Parramatta Eels in the Final.
Why did he come back? Because a signing ban on English players was introduced for Australian RL and he wanted to stake a claim for a place on the 1979 Tour Down Under.
Touring: He also treasures his selection for the 1979 Tour of Australia and New Zealand as well as being named as captain for the 1980 Test series against New Zealand although injury prevented him from either playing or taking up that prestigious office.

Nigel Stephenson

Age: 57.
Born: Dewsbury.
Clubs: Dewsbury, Bradford Northern, Wakefield Trinity, Carlisle, York, Hunslet and Huddersfield.
Retired: 1990.
Rarity: Nigel is one of the few players to have plied his trade on a rugby field in four different decades. He played just one game for Huddersfield in 1990 to chalk up that particular achievement.
Retirement: Like so many other good players of his gener-ation, he put retirement off until

the last possible moment. In the end he collected his last pay packet from the game when he was 39 years old.
What did he do for a job? He started work at ICI in Huddersfield - it became AstraZeneca – and rose to the dizzy heights of a contract manager.
And then? He took early retirement. He and his family had always had a liking for the sun so once he'd finished with his working life, he emigrated to Spain.
Lucky chap: He was, and still is, because he built a house near Alicante and had the life of Riley – swimming pools, the lot.
Wanderlust: But then the Stephenson family remembered their family holidays in Florida, so they upped sticks and re-emigrated to the good 'ol US of A. Today he lives in retirement near Davenport, Florida.
What's the lifestyle like? Hey, Nigel loves it. *"I've got a fantastic home and I live near a great golf course. We've got other attractions like alligators nearby too."*
How's the handicap? *"I started off 24 but the Americans soon got wise to me! But golf has replaced rugby in my life and I play at least three times a week".*
Rugby League. Is he trying to convert the yanks? It would be easier to get Dale Winton to take up the game.

Mike Stephenson

Age: At least 50.
Aka: Stevo.
League era: 1966 – 1978.
Clubs: Dewsbury and Penrith Panthers.
Appearance: Thinning on top and well turned out. Should win Tie Wearer of the Year any time now.

Playing career: Mike was a quality hooker in the Dewsbury team that won the Rugby League Championship in 1973.
So rumour has it: He left behind a promising career in painting and decorating for the flesh pots of Australia. It was reported that after his meeting with the Penrith representatives, he just put down his paint brush at a job and it's still there waiting for him to come back.
Reason for retirement: Injury.
After his playing days: Afterwards he started to build up a massive collection of RL memorabilia and he sent it out on tour around the continent using a specially chartered train as the exhibition centre.
A new career: From Australia, Mike was recruited to write a column for the old 'Rugby Leaguer' newspaper. That kept him in the media spotlight and, when the former BSB satellite broadcaster launched its coverage in 1990, 'Stevo' was recruited to front the service.
Was he a natural in front of the camera? Yes. He was teamed up with Liverpudlian Eddie Hemmings - a position they still fill today. They're like Cannon and Ball, Crockett and Tubbs, Bangers and Mash. Perfect together.
Stevo the Businessman: Mike owns the Rugby League Heritage Centre at the George Hotel in Huddersfield. This extra tourist attraction has been based at the hotel where the famous split from the Rugby Union happened back in August 1895.
Still visiting Down Under? Amazingly Mike still has a wife, family and home back in Sydney. We say surprisingly because he spends nine months a year living in London, where he has a business life as well as his television career.

Anthony Sullivan

DOB: 23 November 1968.
Born: Hull
Clubs: Hull KR, St Helens
Playing era: 1986 – 2003

The blink of an eye: You only saw him when they slowed down the action replays on the big screen. He was fast.

So he went over to the dark side? He had one spell on loan to Cardiff Rugby Union Club before moving there on a permanent basis in August 2001. He was one of the first players from league to win international recognition in union after the 15-a-side code embraced professionalism.

Going for soccer glory: Today Anthony, who lives in Warrington, is living his dream because he has become a Football Association Grade One coach and during mid 2007 he was studying for his Grade Two Qualification.

Why? Because he wants to coach soccer. He could be the next Ferguson.

Sarah or Alex? He's starting small as coach with a Warrington Junior Soccer Club and, who knows, he could win the World Cup as manager of Wales.

Working life: When he was on the books at Hull KR he worked for one of the club's directors and he was a Design Estimator. In other words he went round putting temporary buildings and caravans in the right place.

A bit like the gypsies. What's he doing today? Well for a time he was an independent financial advisor but he switched away from that so that today he works in the building trade where he is a self-styled 'jack of all trades'.

Clive Sullivan MBE

DOB: 1943.
Born: Splott, Cardiff.
Clubs: Hull FC, Hull KR.
Era: 1961 – 1981.
Position: Winger
Appearances: 582.
Game style: Fast, really fast.
Theatre: Clive's life was brought to the stage by writer Dave Windass and was called 'Sully'.
What were the reviews like? Absolutely divine, darling.
So give me the elevator pitch: Only black kid in Welsh village beats racism to unite a city; becomes last rugby league

captain to raise the World Cup, nearly dies in a car crash; but is beaten by cancer aged just 42.
Blimey, tell us about his most famous try: A length of the field effort to secure a 10-10 draw against Australia in Lyon that won the World Cup for the Lions.
I can see that getting the Lloyd Webber treatment: Did I mention when he was teenager he underwent surgery on his shoulders and knees which looked to have ruled out a career in rugby of either code?
I can see it on the West End with Felicity Kendal and Michael Crawford. Any TV stardom for Clive? He was a subject of 'This Is Your Life' in the days when Eamonn Andrews did it.
Those books cost £250 each you know? A month's pay back then
Homage: The main road into Hull from the Humber Bridge is now named after him.
The wind still blows: His son, Anthony Sullivan, went on to have a distinguished career with Hull Kingston Rovers and St Helens.

Clive Sullivan passed away in 1985

Mick Sullivan

Age: 73.
Born: Leeds
Clubs: Huddersfield, Wigan, St Helens, York, Dewsbury, Batley, Junee (Australia).
I thought it was convicts who went to Australia in those days? He was cutting edge was Mick.
Retired: 1970.
Honours: Mick was a player who won everything in the game.
Did he win Miss Dewsbury 1967? No, but he went to Wembley three times - Wigan in 1958 and 1959 and St Helens in

1961 - picking up winners' medals each time.
Working: Like all of the Rugby League professionals of the time Mick had to work and he was a plumber.
Until his big end went: Very funny. He stayed with the trade until he signed for Wigan when he bought a fish and chip shop in Pudsey. His mum and wife ran the business while he played Rugby League. At that time Wigan allowed him to train at Hunslet one night a week to save him having to travel to Central Park.
Did he have a secret recipe for his fish batter? If I told you, I would have to kill you.
Let's move to..: Wigan. He got a job doing repairs at schools and other council buildings.
Back to Yorkshire: Eventually York signed Mick and that saw him change industries again because he then took a pub, the Royal Oak near the Minster. He stayed with York for almost two years and, following a controversial spell with Australian club Junee, he signed for Dewsbury and Batley. He was player coach to Dewsbury and later coached the Batley club.
I am exhausted reading all that. Did he have time to retire? With his playing days over Mick joined the Prison Service and worked at Wakefield Prison. After 17 years in the service he retired and now lives in Dewsbury.

Eddie Szymala

His age is the same as his scrabble score on a triple word score: 53.
Born: Barrow-in-Furness.
Position: Hooker.
Retired: 1983.
Nickname: Smiler.
Retirement: Serious ankle injury.
Fitness fanatic: When he played, he was seriously into body building and built his own gymnasium at home so that he could train on his own patch.
Embarrassing moment: After an international fixture in France, Eddie decided to forgo breakfast and have a lie in. The phone in his room rang and a very French accent on the line wanted to know if was the famous Mr Szymala and could meet him in the hotel lobby for an autograph. Eddie got dressed and went downstairs. The moment he walked into the breakfast room he knew he'd been had because he got a massive cheer from the British players.
Best moments: Being picked for England and Great Britain. *"International call ups always went to players from clubs like Wigan, St Helens, Leeds and Bradford. For a lad from Barrow to get the call up meant you had to play that bit better than other lads. You had to try that little bit harder."*
Did he ever play against Australia? Yes he did the same year but for Barrow. *"We were drawing 2-2 at half time but the Kangaroos ran away with it in the second half."*
Work: Eddie's a fitter by trade and worked in the shipyard at Barrow. Today he's a shot blaster and industrial painter and does the business on atomic powered submarines when they are built at the yard.
Does he ever get tempted to take one out for a spin? He would do but they're a buggar to get parked again.
Was does he think of the Trident upgrade? As long as they need painting he loves them.
Famous friends: Eddie became friends with Brian Barwick who has gone on to a £350,000 a year job as head of the Football Association. Barwick used to interview Eddie on a regular basis as a journalist for the Whitehaven News.

Jimmy Thompson

Age: 58.
Clubs: Featherstone Rovers, Bradford Northern, Carlisle.
Era: 1966 – 1984
Distinctive appearance: Bald head and a headband protecting his ears.
Retirement: Same old story. It was one tackle too far.
And so...: But just as the carpet clippers and fireside were beckoning, in came Bradford Northern coach Peter Fox.
Was somebody needed to bring sand on for the kicker? He persuaded Jimmy he still had some more to offer the game and to sign for Northern.

Did he have any more games in him? Six more glorious years.
Work: Jimmy started life as colliery fitter. First he was based at the area workshops and then Featherstone's Ackton Hall pit – what a team they could have put out during the 1970s – and then after the last national miners' strike in 1984 he moved into the insurance industry. Today he is happily retired and living near Featherstone.
What sort of insurance did he sell? It was the boom times when people could go for personal pensions. Of course he knew lots of team mates who didn't have anything set up at all and they can have a happy retirement thanks to Jimmy.
Daughter: One of them married RL starlet Richard Newlove.
Highlight: Jimmy's a legend because he played on the 1970 tour of Australia and New Zealand and his team remain the last to beat Australia in a series to this day.

David Topliss

Age: 57.
Ahhhh, the Cary Grant of Rugby League. Was he born in Bristol by any coincidence? No, Wakefield.
Clubs: Wakefield Trinity (twice), Hull FC, Oldham. Penrith, Balmain (Australia)
Era: It all came to a sad in the mid-80s.
Sad end? For the fans because he was a true gent and well liked.
Position: Stand off half.
Nickname: Topper.
Retired: 38 years of age.
Working life: After training as a

motor mechanic Dave had his first spell playing in Australia with Penrith. When he came back to the UK he went into business as a plumbers' merchant. Later on he started his own company in the same business
And today? Dave and his partner sold the business several years ago and he's been in semi-retirement ever since. He does work as a sales director for a company called Meadow Pipeline Supplies in Sheffield.
What does he sales direct? The usual thing; stainless steel flanges and valves.
Are they 24-hour? No.
Okay, I'll bear that in mind just in case I need anything.
Hobbies: Playing five-a-side soccer.
Highlights: Top of his list is being on the Hull FC side that beat Widnes in the 1982 Challenge Cup Final replay at Elland Road, Leeds and leading his home-town club Trinity out at Wembley to face Widnes in the 1979 Challenge Cup Final at Wembley. Widnes won that day but Dave was named as Lance Todd Trophy winner as Man of the Match.

Ian Van Bellen

A Dutchman? 'Afraid not. He's from Huddersfield.

Age: 62.

Clubs: Huddersfield (twice), Castleford, Bradford Northern, Fulham, Blackpool, Kent Invicta, Keighley.

Playing era: 1963 – 1984.

Height: Over 6 ft 2.

Trade mark: Bald with flowing long blond hair round the sides. A bit like a baddie from the film 'Die Hard'.

Signature dish: Bullocking runs. If the Spanish ever ran out of bulls to have charging down the back streets of Pamplona

then they could have called up Ian for the job.

End of his playing days: Wear and tear in '84.

The patron saint of job centres: Ian's had loads of jobs.

As what? It ranges from building sites to warehouseman for a Japanese pen manufacturer.

Variety is the spice of life: While he was at Fulham he became a commercial representative selling man hole covers.

Was he good at that? Bearing in mind he couldn't actually fit down them himself, he was one of the best. When he left though he got a nice pen. Even engraved. Something he didn't really need given his previous work record.

Where could I catch up with him today if say I wanted to know the history of man hole covers: He's in semi-retirement living in Huddersfield.

How did he come to sign for Northern? *"One day in the dressing room Neil (Fox) said that "there were three men all going for the two prop positions and that could not continue". "So I said to him 'That means I've got to go doesn't it'. He said it did but added "our kid (Bradford coach Peter Fox) wants you at Bradford". "So I went."*

League today: Ian sees quite a number of the Huddersfield Giants games and is a member of the club's Players' Association.

Kevin Ward

Age: 50.
Born: Wakefield
Clubs: Castleford, Manly
(Australia), St Helens
Era: 1978 - 1993
Position: Prop
**How would I recognise him
on the pitch?** Puffed out chest,
tight shirt with a big heart and a
huge moustache. It was kind of
butch then but a bit gay now. He
was also one of the first players
to wear a head band.
Bad break: Kevin can recall the
exact date when he retired from
playing because he broke his leg
playing for St Helens against

Wigan at Central Park on Good Friday 1993. He was 36.
How is he today? Well, big Kev isn't a spirit you can put down
easily but he was given the option to have his leg amputated or
face living with the pain. He chose to stand on his own two feet
and not have one built for him!
Book: Appropriately enough he had a book on his life called 'No
Pain, No Gain'.
Sense of humour: Even 14 years after his career was
tragically cut short he can still raise smile. He recalls being man
of the match in an Australian game when he played for Manly
and winning a Toyota car. It was too expensive to ship home and
they wouldn't give him the cash instead. So he flew home
without it.
Where is it now? Still in Sydney I guess and home to two
aborigine families.
Working life: Kevin started life on the 'tools', as he puts it, in
a Wakefield-based engineering company but now he's the boss.
Memories: After a 16-year professional playing career Kevin
has a load of highlights to recall but his favourite is winning the
1987 Australian Grand Final with Manly.

Edward Marsden Waring

Who? Eddie Waring to you and me. The great commentator.

DOB: 1910, Dewsbury.

He hardly played rugby league though did he? Without Eddie, there might not be any rugby league. He brought it to TV in the late 50s. Well, before Ray French, and Stevo.

What about playing? He cut his teeth as a manager then went into journalism before launching the phrase 'Up 'n' Under' on the nation.

Who did he write for? He had a column for the Sunday Mirror.

Didn't he do 'It's A Knockout'? He did with (Ha-ha) Stuart Hall, but many league fans didn't like him doing both. They thought he was making the game so trivial that the BBC received a petition signed by 2,000 league fans to have him taken off 'It's A Knockout'.

But he survived? Until 1981 when, at 71 years of age he commentated on his final game. Hull versus Hull KR.

I can feel a tear coming on: Well, sadly he didn't last much longer after that. In 1986, old Eddie aged just 76 went to that early bath in the sky. Buried in his trilby and trademark camel hair coat, his legacy lives on with those who remember the *fil rouge* and the Don Fox miss-kick of 1968.

Home: Leeds. He actually had an office in the Queen's Hotel in the centre of Leeds.

Why? To manage his TV career and be near the train station. He was very much in demand. In his heyday he was on the Morecombe and Wise show and kept Mike Yarwood in a job for years.

David Watkins MBE

Age: He gets his pension.
Born: Blaina, Monmouthshire.
Clubs: Salford, Swinton.
Playing era: 1967 – 1979.
Height: 5 ft 6.
Stature: He was like the boss from Thunderbirds.
Appreciated: Just after his big money signing from Welsh rugby union he missed a vital tackle for Salford and a fan shouted loud enough for the players to hear: *"For goodness sake Watkins, hit 'im with your wallet!"*
Work: When David played in union he worked in the finance industry and remained within it until he retired in 2007.

Staying in rugby: After he finished in Rugby League, David became one of the most outspoken critics of rugby union's ban on former Rugby League personnel being allowed to return to their roots. Following union's professionalism in 1995 David returned to his former union club Newport and during the 1992-1993 season he became the Newport Team manager.
Promoted: His knowledge and passion for the game of rugby football saw David rise to a position of significance at Rodney Parade when he became chairman of Newport.
Cross code: Although a member of the Welsh rugby establishment, David is often to be seen at league games in Wales and in 2006 he, together with Falklands War hero Simon Weston, were made patrons of the Welsh rugby league at a ceremony staged at the Welsh Assembly.
What does that involve? Getting the game accepted into schools across South Wales. So far 24 schools have taken up the sport. Bodes well for the future.
Does Simon Weston like league? He's a union man himself but did watch the 13-man game when he lived in the North-West.
He's doing well: He's also been awarded an honorary degree by the University of Salford.
Do they do PHD's in rugby league? That's the Polytechnic.

Dave Watkinson

Age: 53.
A Cross between: Eddie Large and Kurt Sorensen.
Born: York.
Clubs: Hull KR, Dewsbury.
Playing era: 1977 – 1990.
In a nutshell: Gritty.
Meaning? You wouldn't want to meet him up a dark alley.
Working life: Dave worked in the construction industry as a building contractor and he still works in it today.
He constructs large objects instead of knocking them down which is what he did as a player: You got it. He also had the rugby league moustache.

Sport: Like so many other former professional Dave's a keen golfer and his handicap is 16 and he likes to go fishing now and again

Lowlights: Being picked for the 1979 tour of Australia and New Zealand, but missing out on the 1984 tour Down Under because he had broken a leg.

Going to the game: Occasionally Dave goes through from his home in York to watch Hull KR but today is more or less an armchair follower of the professional sport. He does follow the affairs of the amateur game in York and can often be seen on the sidelines when the well known York club Heworth take the field.

A job in the game: Dave did entertain ambitions of going into Rugby League team management and he was assistant coach at York to Derek Foster for a spell. He was offered the first team coaching role with the Minstermen but the club apparently changed their mind at the last moment.

Derek Whitehead

DOB: 14 February 1944.

A war baby: Swinton had many.

A good old fashioned rugby league name isn't it: Yes, not many guys called Derek these days.

Clubs: Swinton, Oldham, Warrington.

Era: 1961 - 1980.

Position: Full-back or wing three-quarter.

Party piece: Had one of the best side steps ever seen in Rugby League. He used to string a number of them together and, occasionally, opponents worked out what was happening and on the third side step a defender was perfectly positioned to send him crashing.

He wasn't at Oldham for long? No, he left after a year. His transfer money was needed to pay wages that week.

Did he regret leaving? No. The timing was great since Alex Murphy was the new player-coach and it was the start of a golden era for the club.

Work: Derek was a butcher for 25 years. After that he went to be a driver for international courier company DHL but now he works for a Mancunian Toyota car dealer delivering new cars to their outlets and customers.

Might I see him on the motorway begging for a lift? Possibly. If you do, pick him up and chat about the old days.

Wembley Magic: Derek won the Lance Todd Trophy as the man of the match in the 1974 Challenge Cup Final at Wembley when Warrington beat Featherstone Rovers 24-9.

What were his heroics that day? *"I got it because I kept Warrington in the game with my goal kicking. It was an incredible experience."*

John Woods

Age: 50.
Born: Leigh.
Clubs: Leigh, Bradford Northern, Warrington, Rochdale Hornets.
Era: 1975 – 1990.
Talent: One of the most gifted players of his generation.
Fault: Probably stayed at his home-town club of Leigh for far too long when a place at a glamour club may have taken him further.
Work: When he left school one of John's first jobs was as a rat catcher but by the time he became a well known player he

was a Heavy Goods Vehicle driver. And he's stayed in the driving game ever since.

And now? Today, he's still behind a wheel but working for the police as a driver doing all kinds of jobs for the force including moving their civilian workforce about Greater Manchester.

Modesty: Considering what an amazing Rugby League star he was for so many years, John remains a quiet, unassuming guy who's happy with his lot and grateful for his Rugby League career.

Today: John's main interest in life is fishing. He's a pure pleasure coarse fisherman who doesn't bother with competitions.

His favourite memories: Being picked to play for Great Britain in 1979 and winning the League title with Alex Murphy's Leigh team in 1982.

Any regrets? When he didn't sign for Hull FC in 1980 and they went on to reach the Challenge Cup Final that year.